Guide to Lancashire

by

Ken Lawson

Bird photography by
Stan Craig A.R.P.S. and
Bob Marsh A.R.P.S.

Lancashire County Books, 1994

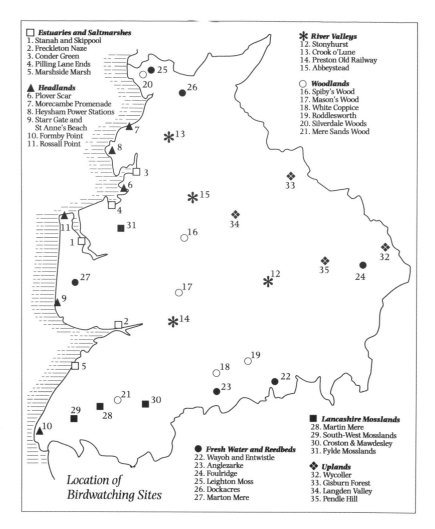

Estuaries and Saltmarshes
1. Stanah and Skippool
2. Freckleton Naze
3. Conder Green
4. Pilling Lane Ends
5. Marshside Marsh

Headlands
6. Plover Scar
7. Morecambe Promenade
8. Heysham Power Stations
9. Starr Gate and St Anne's Beach
10. Formby Point
11. Rossall Point

River Valleys
12. Stonyhurst
13. Crook o'Lune
14. Preston Old Railway
15. Abbeystead

Woodlands
16. Spiby's Wood
17. Mason's Wood
18. White Coppice
19. Roddlesworth
20. Silverdale Woods
21. Mere Sands Wood

Fresh Water and Reedbeds
22. Wayoh and Entwistle
23. Anglezarke
24. Foulridge
25. Leighton Moss
26. Dockacres
27. Marton Mere

Lancashire Mosslands
28. Martin Mere
29. South-West Mosslands
30. Croston & Mawdesley
31. Fylde Mosslands

Uplands
32. Wycoller
33. Gisburn Forest
34. Langden Valley
35. Pendle Hill

Location of Birdwatching Sites

A Birdwatchers' Guide to Lancashire
by Ken Lawson
First published 1994

Text © Ken Lawson, 1994
Published by Lancashire County Books, 143 Corporation Street, Preston
Typeset in Monotype Photina by Carnegie Publishing Ltd, Preston
Printed by Cambridge University Press

British Library Cataloguing-in-Publication Data

A catalogue record for this book is available from the British Library
ISBN 1-871236-32-0

Contents

Introduction

Bird Habitat in Lancashire

Lancashire encompasses a wide variety of habitats which makes it a good region for many different kinds of birds and hence for bird-watchers too. Land altitudes range from just below mean sea level to 627m, while vegetation covers every variation between the open plains of intensive agriculture to dense forests. Meanwhile the damp climate ensures that water, the one essential for all forms of animal life, is seldom far away. This diversity provides sustenance and shelter for a profusion of breeding birds and, although the east coast of Britain is better placed for arrivals of eurasian migrants, Lancashire's coastal areas do attract some interesting migratory species. In addition, the generally milder conditions on the west coast render it attractive to large numbers of wintering birds avoiding the colder weather on the other side of the Pennine chain and on the continent.

The area covered by this guide broadly follows the current Lancashire boundary except in relation to the southern coastal region where a common sense line, following the River Alt to the sea, is adopted rather than the one defined for political expediency. My main departure from the traditional mould of regional bird guides is the grouping of sites by habitat rather than physical position and the inclusion of a section on each habitat type. This represents an attempt to provide a more sound ecological basis for the information presented although there is inevitably some overlap between different classes of habitat. Most species use a variety of aspects within a chosen area and examples of common requirements for birds are the availability of fresh water for drinking and bathing; foods of various kinds; and nesting and roosting sites. A suitable habitat needs to include all such features in reasonably close proximity. Indeed the very problem with the habitat approach is that the best sites are those which do contain such a good mix that it is difficult to decide which is the most important habitat feature. Thus when a stream enhances the value of a woodland habitat it causes overlap with the river valley classification which in turn has potential for confusion with the uplands. Similarly

1

many Lancashire reservoirs are surrounded by woods sometimes at an intermediate altitude or in an exposed position which confers a degree of upland character; while on the coast, headlands tend to merge into more estuarine stretches without always a sharp distinction and may even be backed by mossland regions. When in doubt I have tried to base the classification on the locally significant bird species to be found at the site in question.

Scrubland is an important habitat for many species of birds, especially at migration times, yet has not been allotted a chapter of its own partly because scrub is so often present as an element in virtually every other kind of habitat and partly on account of its transient nature. Books such as this inevitably become out of date: land use is constantly changing and whilst some good habitats are created, others are destroyed or at least radically altered. Likewise bird species can experience changing fortunes, sometimes linked with such changes in the use of land, whereas in other cases populations may be subject to natural cyclic variations often associated with food supply. These two factors mean that good places to see particular species can change over time.

Choice of Sites

The choice of sites is necessarily a personal one and birdwatchers with some knowledge of their local areas may notice some omissions. However what I have tried to do is include a representative selection of sites for each habitat in such a way as to cover all the special birds of the region as well as the more widespread species. In some cases this aim has been tempered by the need for confidentiality as to the breeding sites of a very few species which are particularly vulnerable to human activities, and so are not discussed other than in general terms. In the main, the chosen sites are pleasant places to be, with some sort of scenic value: rubbish tips (for example Salt Ayre at Lancaster) and sewage works can be good places to see some species, such as glaucous and Iceland gulls or water pipits, but access is often a problem. Permits may be available from North West Water for visiting some sewage works but in Lancashire the conversion to modern filter beds has made them far less attractive to birds. Urban and suburban habitats have also been excluded which is not to imply that they are of no use to birds. The sparrowhawk population has increased dramatically since the withdrawal of most persistent pesticides and the relaxation of deliberate persecution, with the result that

The variety of bird species to be found in Wycoller Country Park reflects the range of habitats represented, from upland river valley with wooded patches to rough grassland and moors.

these birds are now regularly seen in predominantly built-up areas such as Preston. For true beginners there is no better place to start birdwatching than wherever is nearest to hand which is often their own back garden. I know of no more reliable site for tree sparrows than my own garden and that is simply because they breed nearby and I feed them in winter. When a little more experience has been gained, organized nature reserves are also good places to watch birds because there are often wall charts to aid identification and relative experts on hand to help.

Species Listed in Sites

The lists of birds are largely based on my own observations and hopefully represent what is realistically achievable for an average birdwatcher. This means that they are not exhaustive: for example tawny owls may be resident anywhere with mature trees. To confirm their presence night visits are usually required and so they are probably to be found at many sites other than those identified. A similar consideration applies to woodcock which are most reliably seen on their spring roding flights at dawn and dusk. Some species are so widespread that, to avoid their being on the list for virtually every site, they have simply been excluded altogether. A good example is the swift which can be seen feeding in summer at all altitudes from sea level to the tops of the Lakeland fells: indifferent to urbanization and oblivious of people they just follow their insect food wherever it takes them. Meanwhile the wren is an equivalent example of a resident species with the ultimate in catholic choice of habitat from almost bare hillsides in the uplands to fairly dense forests anywhere.

Seasons and Tides

If there is a logical start for the birdwatching year I think of it as the beginning of the spring migration for this is when our summer visitors return home to breed again. Migration can depend to a marked degree on the weather but this is far too complex a subject for full treatment in a guide of this nature. However it can be said that, from the British birdwatcher's point of view, the ideal conditions for spring migration are when an anticyclone (high pressure) is settled over southern Europe, feeding wave upon wave of migrants through to the north, some of them overshooting their normal breeding range by several hundred miles or even more. This is the sort of time to see a hoopoe for example and, although the chances are obviously greater in southern England, such rarities do occasionally reach Lancashire. On the other hand it is the autumn migration season when inexperienced juvenile migrants sometimes go astray and hence almost anything can turn up.

After the frantic breeding season there is a lull, at least as far as the songbirds are concerned, from the end of June onwards when many adult birds are in moult and keep well hidden. Nevertheless the return migration has begun by the end of July for passerines and even earlier for waders. Indeed one occasionally sees an odd wader, presumed to be a migrant, in late June or early July and wonders which way it is going and whether it is perhaps wondering the same thing! The situation is further complicated by birds which actually spend the summer here while most of their kind are breeding further north or in a different habitat. Often these are young birds, below the normal breeding age for the species, although their plumage may resemble that of adults: kittiwake and several kinds of wader spring to mind as examples. These sort of considerations affect the way in which the various seasons indicated in the site information are to be interpreted. For instance merlin may return to Marshside Marsh (see chapter one) from the hill country as early as August and the first golden plovers from July, so although they are both listed as winter visitors, this is not designed to be taken too literally. Under each site the term 'winter visitors' is used in a broader sense meaning outside the breeding season for the species concerned, that is to say not generally present throughout the year. Both the 'winter visitors' and 'breeding season' designations may be taken to include the surrounding migration periods as well.

By November most birds are settled in their winter quarters, subsequent movements being mainly local and prompted by changes in the weather. Cold weather causes birds to move nearer the coast where the warming maritime influence reduces overall energy requirements and water is generally less subject to freezing. This applies especially to birds which obtain their food from the water but all species need a source of fresh water and some birds of prey have an added reason for moving to the coast in that they must follow their source of food. On the other hand prolonged periods of gales can bring birds which usually winter at sea, such as divers, inland in search of shelter. In some winters there will be an influx of a particular species which is caused by a shortage of food in their normal wintering ranges and is particularly characteristic of those species of finch (including crossbill, siskin, redpoll and brambling) which rely on trees with a marked fluctuation in the seed crop from year to year: waxwing are in a similar situation but with regard to berries. The general severity of the winter in continental Europe, especially where food is unavailable due to thick snow or freezing conditions, affects other birds which may then visit Britain in greater numbers than usual.

Tides are so important in governing the behaviour of shorebirds that a current set of tide tables (which may be obtained from shops selling fishing tackle) is necessary for efficient birdwatching in coastal regions. In general higher tides bring the birds closer but some tides may be too big for a particular site, for example by submerging a feeding or roosting area for waders which must then move elsewhere.

Listening to Birds

Birds are much easier to locate and identify if one has a working knowledge of the different sounds they make. A few are signals produced by non-vocal means, for example the drumming of a snipe or a woodpecker, and there are some incidental sounds such as the tap-ping of a feeding woodpecker or nuthatch, or the wing beats of swans passing close overhead. However, the vast majority of the audible clues are of vocal origin and are designed for communication with other birds. Closely related species which are very similar in appear-ance tend to be easily distinguishable by voice. The classic example is chiffchaff and willow warbler whose territorial songs are clearly different, avoiding interbreeding between them which would eventually result in their becoming one species by hybridization. As a group, warblers are generally secretive birds but in spring, when the males are establishing territories and advertising for mates, they cannot afford to be so shy: thus springtime offers the best chance of seeing them, especially in con-junction with song. More than any other species this seems to apply to lesser whitethroats which, if not seen soon after they arrive in this coun-try, can easily be missed for the whole year. Once the songs and calls of the common birds can be instantly recognized by voice, the brain will learn to automatically filter out these sounds allowing one to notice anything out of the ordinary more readily.

Welfare of Birds

With birdwatching as an increasingly popular hobby, it is important to minimize disturbance to both birds and their habitat. Some species more or less ignore people while others are very wary and even within a species there are clear differences in tolerance levels of human pres-ence. A standing silhouette against the skyline is the surest way of scaring birds so use whatever cover may be available. Do not ap-proach too closely: advance warning signs of anxiety amongst birds include ceasing to feed and looking up and around instead. Flushing birds is often unnecessary and causes them to waste energy which in some circumstances may have an impact on their breeding success or chances of individual survival. Also have consideration for other birdwatchers and always respect landowners' rights to privacy. It seems only fair that those who derive so much enjoyment from birds should strive to make some contribution to their welfare and future prospects. At one level the key to local conservation is raising public awareness of the bounty of wildlife in Lancashire, of which birds form an important part.

1

Estuaries and Saltmarshes

Lancashire is endowed with a long coastline which is predominantly sandy, with mud in the river estuaries. There are pebbles and shingle in places, but not much in the way of rock or cliffs. This chapter is concerned mainly with the tidal area of mud, sand and the adjoining saltmarsh, which is reached only by the higher tides and is often used by birds for roosting at high water. The saltmarsh is very significant in area, about ten per cent of the British total, but it is the mud and sand flats that are of paramount importance to birds. The Ribble and Lune estuaries and Morecambe Bay are accordingly designated as SSSIs (Sites of Special Scientific Interest) totalling over 47,000 hectares, of which just under half is within Lancashire, much of Morecambe Bay being in Cumbria. Both the Ribble Estuary and Morecambe Bay have also been proposed as Ramsar sites and SPAs (Special Protection Areas) but are currently awaiting such designation.

The reason for the importance of this habitat is that the intertidal zone is an immensely productive biological system, incredibly rich in invertebrate animals which provide food for many thousands of waders in particular. Morecambe Bay is second in Britain only to The Wash, in its importance for waders, and the Ribble Estuary, with an autumn peak of over 100,000 waders, is in third place. More specifically the Ribble Estuary holds more sanderling and black-tailed godwit than any other British site. It is also second in importance for wildfowl in Britain, again after The Wash. The pink-footed geese are the main reason for this assessment although the estuary regularly holds more than ten per cent of the British population of wigeon as well. Among the ducks, shelduck are the most closely associated with estuaries throughout the year and pintail also show a certain affinity for muddy situations. The British Isles occupy a unique position on a main migration route for waders and wildfowl breeding in the Arctic from Canada to Siberia. Hence these myriads of birds all converge on our coasts either to spend the whole winter or to build up their energy reserves for the next stage in their flight further south.

Outside the breeding season there is reduced territorial behaviour among birds which enables them to feed close together in flocks and thus exploit locally abundant food sources more efficiently. This applies to passerines feeding on the seeds and fruit of saltmarsh plants, which mature only after the breeding season is over, as well as to waders and wildfowl. As breeding habitat, on the other hand, the usefulness of saltmarsh is limited by periodic flooding from the sea. It is however the preferred nesting ground of redshanks, whose chicks float and so endure tides which inundate the nest. Other species to make significant use of Lancashire saltmarshes for breeding include oystercatcher, lapwing, skylark, meadow pipit and common tern. The last breeds in colonies on the Lune marshes and Banks Marsh, on the Ribble Estuary. Snipe, curlew and teal can also breed on saltmarshes and especially those of the North-West, including Lancashire. In addition, two particularly interesting species, dunlin and wheatear, regularly breed in very small numbers on Carnforth Marsh.

Most of Lancashire's saltmarshes are grazed by farm stock, the exceptions being Barnaby Sands Marsh and Burrows Marsh, on the eastern side of the Wyre Estuary, which are designated as SSSIs for this reason. The effects of grazing on birds, however, are rather complicated. Heavy grazing is likely to be detrimental by making the vegetation too short to provide effective cover for breeding birds and causing excessive disturbance to birds at any time of year. An absence of grazing, on the other hand, tends to result in clumps of coarse vegetation which renders the habitat less suitable for waders, ducks and breeding terns and gulls, although it can favour passerines such as meadow pipit and skylark. Also the supply of invertebrates in the soil may be increased by the extra nutrients provided by the droppings of herbivores and this is helpful to breeding waders for example. The overall conclusion is that moderate grazing has some beneficial effects for various species of birds.

One of the major potential threats to intertidal habitat comes from the possibility of constructing tidal barrages to generate electricity. Lancashire is no exception in this matter and various schemes have been proposed. The idea of a barrage across Morecambe Bay has had a high public profile for many years and the bay is still under threat as new options continue to be forwarded. Other sites on the Lune Estuary and particularly the Wyre Estuary have also been suggested. The latter currently appears the most promising and is the subject of a recent preliminary feasibility study. This estuary is noted especially for its migrant flock of some two hundred black-tailed godwits (which represents about four per cent of the British population) almost half of which overwinter here. It is widely acknowledged that insufficient work has yet been carried out to

*Lapwings are a common sight in Lancashire and, although
not restricted to coastal areas, can be found on saltmarshes
throughout the year. (B. Marsh.)*

fully assess the likely effects of the scheme on the wildlife of the area
and a comprehensive environmental impact study is essential before
any final decision is reached.

Given the right conditions estuaries can be magical places for birdwatching: the spectacle of massed flight from the waders, especially
knot which assemble in vast flocks; the sheer number of birds wheeling and turning in unison, is simply awe inspiring. Being in the right
place at the right time is as important as ever but fortunately the
times are fairly predictable by the use of tide tables. The life of a
shorebird is governed almost solely by the tides rather than by night
and day. The usual pattern is to feed, by probing the exposed mud,
when the tide is out and to conserve energy by roosting (sleeping)
when the tide is in. However, lapwings and golden plovers are unusual among the waders in that they tend to feed (often together)
further inland on flooded fields at high tide and hence roost at low
tide. Some wildfowl also follow this pattern while gulls, being more
adaptable in their feeding habits, may roost at different states of tide

depending on local feeding conditions or independently of tides if feeding inland, for example at a rubbish tip.

Many waders feed on or near the shoreline and on an incoming tide they will be pushed ever closer to a stationary observer. By high water on a 'spring' tide (the higher set which occur on a fortnightly cycle) the birds will be resting on their traditional roost sites. Estuaries are by their nature very open sites and birds react especially to a human silhouette against the sky. The trick is to get close enough for adequate observation without flushing the birds: this is easiest if you carry a telescope which allows good views without needing to approach too closely.

Waders are renowned for being one of the most difficult groups of birds to identify specifically. Adult birds in breeding dress are generally quite distinctive but not often seen as they breed mostly in the Arctic. It is the winter-plumaged birds and juveniles in autumn which cause the problems. Most people, unless they see waders very regularly, need a few minutes to adjust each time: 'getting your eye in' is the perfect expression for this. However there are some basic pointers to help speed up the process. Sanderling always seem to be paler than any of the other waders, with sharply contrasting black legs and bill, and they run along the tideline with 'clockwork' legs and a characteristic horizontal stance. The most plentiful of the small shorebirds are often dunlin, which look fairly 'ordinary', but their identity may be confirmed by checking the slight downturn at the tip of the bill. Dunlin can be surprisingly variable, especially in size, part of the reason being that there are often birds of different geographical races present together. On waders in general, look for traces of breeding plumage: hints of many such features are even present on juvenile birds. The calls of waders are handy to know but, with so many species present simultaneously, can be difficult to learn 'in the field'.

The presence of large numbers of birds on estuarine habitats in winter inevitably attracts raptors that commonly prey on other birds. Peregrine and merlin are the two such species most closely associated with estuaries and saltmarsh in this way, but a sparrowhawk may occasionally be seen hunting over this kind of habitat as well. The behaviour of waders and other flocks of birds is often indicative of a bird of prey in the vicinity. Especially when a flock rises and wheels sharply from one place and then, moments later, from somewhere nearby, it is sometimes possible to trace the path of a raptor long before (or after) the bird itself is visible. However, birds may react in a similar way to disturbance from a heron or a dog. Kestrels are often seen hunting in all kinds of open habitats, including those in this chapter, but their usual prey is small mammals which they locate by maintaining a hovering position. Adaptability is the key to their success, however, and they may on occasion hunt small birds. Other avian hunters of mammals which typically resort to saltmarsh in winter are hen harriers and short-eared owls. Like merlins and peregrines they generally breed in the uplands and spend much of the winter on the coast, especially when the weather is cold.

Stanah and Skippool

Location

O.S. Landranger Series sheet 102 (Preston & Blackpool) grid reference SD355431.

On the western bank of the Wyre Estuary forming part of the peninsular which terminates at Fleetwood. From the A585(T) to Fleetwood turn off right onto the B5412 to Thornton at the roundabout just by The River Wyre hotel (which is 1km after the junction with the A588 to Knott End and Lancaster). For Skippool Creek (see below) turn immediately right again down Wyre Road and park in the gravel car park on the left after 500m, but for Stanah continue for 1.9km and there turn right by a church on a sweeping left-hand bend. Follow this road to reach Stanah Country Park in 1.2km.

Access

Large car park at Stanah; alternative at Skippool Creek (grid reference SD357410). Stanah Country Park is on a regular circular bus route from Thornton and Cleveleys. Access along the Wyre Way (public footpath) both up and down the river. A high tide will cover the feeding and roosting areas for waders so, on a moderately large tide of around 9m, aim to arrive about 1½ hours in advance of the published time of high water at Fleetwood.

Facilities

Wyreside Ecology Centre with a wealth of local information. Toilets including provision for the disabled.

Habitat

River estuary, tidal creeks, saltmarsh, scrub and hedgerows.

These knot are roosting until the endless twice-daily rhythm of tides once more uncovers their rich feeding grounds. (B. Marsh.)

Birds

Any time of year: grey heron, shelduck, sparrowhawk, kestrel, oystercatcher, collared dove, greenfinch, goldfinch, linnet.

Breeding season: whitethroat.

Winter visitors: cormorant, goldeneye, golden plover, grey plover, lapwing, knot, dunlin, snipe, black-tailed godwit, bar-tailed godwit, curlew, redshank, common gull, skylark, meadow pipit, rock pipit, redwing, brambling.

Passage migrants: common tern.

Given the appropriate tidal conditions, a good variety of waders including **black-tailed godwit** can usually be seen on the section of estuary by the car park at Stanah. The strip of saltmarsh along the near bank of the river, overlooked by the embankment, is frequented by **snipe** and a roving flock of **linnets** in winter. However there is more to Stanah than just the estuary birds, indeed one of my most vividrecollections for this spot is of a fantastically close view of a **sparrowhawk** as it gradually soared away after an unsuccessful hunting attempt. A bird feeding area around the back of the information centre and the adjacent small areas of scrub are possible places for a few winter **brambling**, while other songbirds might be found in the hedgerow along the Wyre Way down-river, towards the ICI works. There is a hide a short way down this footpath but it is kept locked: if interested enquire at the information centre about the availability of a key.

At the far end of the car park embankment the Wyre Way continues up-river to Skippool Creek (3km). There is a good gravel path all the way but in places it may be covered by the highest tides and the intermediate stretch may be less rewarding for birds. Skippool Creek is another interesting area where many of the same species are likely to be seen but it is more favoured by **herons** and even the occasional **little egret** has been seen in recent summers.

Freckleton Naze

Location

O.S. Landranger Series sheet 102 (Preston & Blackpool) grid reference SD432283.

On the north bank of the Ribble Estuary by the confluence of the River Dow and opposite that of the Douglas. Leave the A584 heading towards Lytham at the roundabout onto the old road into Freckleton. Turn left at the traffic lights on the main street and then right in 350m, along Naze Lane East, following signs to Naze Lane Industrial Estate. Park after 600m on rough ground on the left between the road and the gateway to the Poolside Boat Centre.

Access

Backtrack along the road for a short distance to the public footpath which is part of the Lancashire Coastal Way and follow it to the right, away from the road. A telescope is necessary for this site. Strong sunlight at around midday impairs viewing conditions.

Habitat

Estuary, river confluences, open water, scrub, gardens, grazing land.

Birds

Any time of year:　little grebe, grey heron, kestrel, grey partridge, oystercatcher, collared dove, great spotted woodpecker, goldfinch, linnet.

Winter visitors:　cormorant, pink-footed goose, shelduck, wigeon, teal, goldeneye, golden plover, grey plover, lapwing, curlew, redshank, great black-backed gull, skylark, goldcrest.

Passage migrants:　black-tailed godwit, spotted redshank, green-shank, common sandpiper.

The Ribble Estuary is a difficult region to work because the large areas of saltmarsh are indented by so many creeks that a sufficiently close approach is prevented in most places. This is an unusual estuary site in that the main vantage point is an elevated platform overlooking an area of saltmarsh by a river confluence where a bar of sand is exposed at low tide in a predominantly muddy estuary situation. Although the main purpose of a visit to this site is to view a small part of the Ribble Estuary, the initial walk through scrub and farmland, parallel to the River Dow, may produce woodland birds such as **great spotted woodpecker** besides other species on the way. After a while the scrub on the bank of the Dow gives way to a steep meadow (a good spot for butterflies in summer) giving views over open water (variously referred to as the Naze Pool or Freckleton Flash) on the opposite side of the river. The pool is frequented by **little grebes** and **herons** while, alongside the **redshanks** which can be seen all around this area, there might be **greenshank** on migration. In winter ducks such as **goldeneye** and a few of the more common **shelduck** and **teal** sometimes use the pool as well as the adjacent stretch of the Dow. Freckleton also seems to be on a regular flight path for **pink-footed geese** from the Fylde to the southern mossland region, perhaps Martin Mere.

Follow the waymarked footpath to the triangulation point at Naze Mount to view the Ribble Estuary at its confluence with the Douglas. There is no danger of disturbing any estuary birds from here but a telescope is absolutely essential to make any sense of the waders from this distance. There may be **golden plover** amongst the **lapwing** flock while easier to pick out are **curlew**, on account of their larger size, and the striking **oystercatchers**. The confluence attracts passage waders including **spotted redshank** and **greenshank**, especially in late summer and is also noted as a gathering point for **cormorants** in autumn and winter.

Conder Green

Location

O.S. Landranger Series sheet 102 (Preston & Blackpool) grid reference SD457561.

At the confluence of the River Conder with the Lune Estuary, Conder Green is on the A588 between Lancaster and Cockerham about 6km south of Lancaster. Turn off to the west by the Stork Inn and follow this single-track road for 400m to the car park.

Access

Large car park; access on public roads and part of the Lancashire Coastal Way. Low to mid tide is best.

Facilities

Toilets including provision for the disabled. The Stork Inn.

Habitat

River estuaries with good quality water; saltmarsh; scrub.

Birds

Any time of year: grey heron, shelduck, grey partridge, oyster-catcher, lapwing, curlew, redshank, collared dove, kingfisher, skylark, meadow pipit, green-finch, goldfinch, linnet, reed bunting.

Breeding season: sedge warbler.

Winter visitors: cormorant, wigeon, teal, golden plover, snipe, great black-backed gull.

Passage migrants: curlew sandpiper, dunlin, ruff, black-tailed godwit, green sandpiper, common sandpiper, turnstone.

With its contorted meanders and multitudinous creeks and channels, this is a microcosm of an estuarine river system, complete with an element of saltmarsh, all compressed into a few hundred metres. The widest variety of wading species use this site during migration periods, especially in the autumn which for waders can mean any time from mid July until about mid October. Conder Green is noted for being one of the best spots in Lancashire for **curlew sandpipers** on passage. To the wading birds it represents a low-water feeding area rather than a high-tide roosting point and for the birdwatcher it is quite suitable for a relatively brief visit while on the way to somewhere else.

From the car park walk back along the Lancashire Coastal Way, which for this stretch is a disused railway line, to the bridge over the Conder. As well as being treated to fairly close views of any **waders** feeding on the surrounding mud of the Conder Estuary, this is a good vantage point over the Lune Estuary. However, most of the birds on the Lune are usually on the far side of the channel which means that they move yet further away as the tide comes in. Hence a telescope would be useful here, even for the larger species such as **cormorants** and **great black-backed gulls**. It may be worth continuing along the coastal way towards Glasson to cover more of the Lune Estuary: birds likely to be seen from this section include sizeable winter flocks of **golden plover** and **wigeon**. If you reach Glasson, the small marina there deserves a look if only for closer views of **cormorants** roosting on the wooden jetty.

Back at Conder Green walk along the road towards the Stork Inn. **Redshank** and **curlew** are usually widely distributed in the various muddy creeks while **linnets** often gather on the roofs of the buildings on the left. Turn right at the main road but cross over to avoid flushing the flock of **teal** which always seem to be roosting on the muddy bend close to the road. Do not neglect the quiet minor road on the left which allows coverage of the Conder at just about its tidal limit. Approach the stream cautiously so as not to disturb any **snipe** quietly feeding on the river bed. Although rather busy at times, the B5290 to Glasson (just beyond the main road bridge over the Conder) offers views around a meander and parts of channels which are hidden from other directions.

Pilling Lane Ends

Location

O.S. Landranger Series sheet 102 (Preston & Blackpool) grid reference SD414494.

On the north coast of the Fylde along the southern edge of Morecambe Bay. From Stake Pool on the A588 (near Pilling) continue north along this road towards Cockerham for about 1.5km until the Lane Ends Amenity Area is signposted on the left. The entrance to the car park is then in 200m on the right.

Pintail are winter visitors to Lancashire and may be seen at coastal locations as well as on inland fresh waters. (S. Craig.)

Access

From Easter to Christmas one is permitted to walk along the embankment to the west (left) only (but dogs are not allowed). Please observe the notices and keep off the saltmarsh itself. These restrictions are to minimize disturbance to vulnerable wildlife. In view of these arrangements the most rewarding visits are at the highest tides when the birds are pushed up onto the marsh and thus nearer. Even so a telescope will still be required for good views of most birds. In practice there is excessive disturbance on fine summer days, including thoughtless people picnicking on the saltmarsh.

Habitat

Part of a continuous belt of tidal sandflats and saltmarsh with tidal creeks; lakes and some recently planted mixed scrub.

Birds

Any time of year: shelduck, oystercatcher, lapwing, redshank, skylark, goldfinch, linnet.

Winter visitors: little grebe, cormorant, pink-footed goose, brent goose, wigeon, teal, pintail, goldeneye, merlin, peregrine, golden plover, grey plover, knot, dunlin, ruff, snipe, curlew, spotted redshank, greenshank, meadow pipit.

Passage migrants: wheatear.

This is one of the most reliable spots in Lancashire for wintering **brent geese**, a very few of which often graze out on the saltmarsh along with moderately small flocks of **pink-footed geese**. It is worth distinguishing between the two races of brent geese: the birds at this site usually belong to the dark-bellied race. By contrast large numbers of **waders** assemble along this stretch of coastline which in turn encourages the attendance of birds of prey such as **merlin**. These smallest of British falcons regularly perch on posts to survey the open ground over which they hunt in dashing low flight. The perching habit together with the open aspects make them reasonably easy to see, if somewhat distantly, although they are well camouflaged and hence easily overlooked. At the opposite extreme, **shelduck** always seem to be in evidence and their boldly patterned plumage makes them stand out even at a distance. The more westerly of the two small lakes has a more intricate shape affording some shelter for the odd **goldeneye** or **little grebe**.

At migration times, in addition to the expected **wheatears**, rarities are occasionally found, particularly in autumn. One time there were two **Richard's pipits** feeding beside the common **meadow pipits** in the long grass, noticeable when they stood boldly upright like miniature mistle thrushes. Meanwhile a **buff-breasted sandpiper** was visible intermittently around the saltmarsh creeks, again showing rather different feeding behaviour from any of the surrounding, more common waders. On the other hand, in late July a previous year, a **Pacific golden plover** was amongst the flock of **golden plovers** and posed a much more tricky identification problem.

Marshside Marsh

Location

O.S. Landranger Series sheet 102 (Preston & Blackpool) grid reference SD352205.

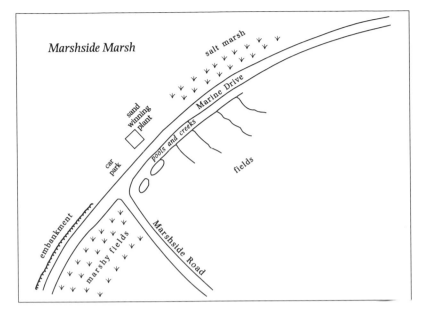

Just north of Southport on the southern edge of the Ribble Estuary (hence I have ignored the nonsense of its being included in Merseyside rather than Lancashire). Approaching Southport from the Preston direction on the A565(T), take the third exit (Marine Drive) at the roundabout on the outskirts of the town. Continue around the sweep of the bend by Crossens Marsh until reaching the sand winning plant after 2.6km. Immediately afterwards is the entrance to a car park on the right.

Access

Ample parking space in the rough gravel car park just south of the sand winning plant. Although part of this land is classified as a National Nature Reserve, be prepared for occasional wildfowling activity which is still allowed on a controlled basis.

Habitat

Sandy coast; large expanse of saltmarsh; extensive area of grazing marsh which floods in winter; permanent pool.

Birds

Any time of year: grey heron, shelduck, shoveler, kestrel, grey partridge, oystercatcher, lapwing, ruff, snipe, redshank, skylark, goldfinch, linnet, reed bunting.

Breeding season: sedge warbler, whitethroat.

Winter visitors: little grebe, Bewick's swan, bean goose, pink-footed goose, white-fronted goose, snow goose, barnacle goose, brent goose, wigeon, teal, pintail, hen harrier, sparrowhawk, merlin, peregrine, water rail, golden plover, grey plover, knot, sanderling, dunlin, black-tailed godwit, bar-tailed godwit, curlew, turnstone, common gull, great black-backed gull, stock dove, short-eared owl, meadow pipit, rock pipit, greenfinch, twite.

Passage migrants: garganey, ringed plover, little stint, curlew sandpiper, whimbrel, wood sandpiper, common sandpiper, Arctic skua, common tern, Arctic tern, little tern, sand martin, wheatear.

This must be one of the richest places in the region for wintering and migrant birds outside an organized nature reserve. It is closely associated with Martin Mere (see chapter six) and birds regularly commute between the two sites, the direct flight line being only 9km. For example the flocks of wildfowl such as geese which roost overnight at Martin Mere for safety often feed at Marshside or the saltmarsh further out into the Ribble Estuary.

Along with Martin Mere, I have found Marshside the best place for seeing **merlin**, **peregrine** and other birds of prey once the breeding season is over. To the north-east of the sand winning plant, the coastal road divides the saltmarsh from the fields inland. Falcons regularly use the habitats on both sides and merlins especially are apt to perch on posts (which are in ample supply all around) allowing detailed viewing with the aid of a telescope. **Kestrels** likewise are often seen on the fence-posts and post-breeding concentrations of mainly young kestrels in this area may reach well into double figures. Sometimes flocks of finches obligingly gather on the fences near the road and in winter **twite** may be located in this way. **Hen harriers** and **short-eared owls** are more likely to be seen hunting over the saltmarsh than the inland side of the road while the reverse is perhaps true of **sparrowhawks**.

Due to the combination of salt and fresh water habitats this is a wonderful area for maximum variety of waders. The species broadly separate into those which prefer the sandy shoreline, such as **bar-tailed godwit**, **knot**, **sanderling** and **grey plover**, and those of the damp fields, including **black-tailed godwit**, **ruff** and large winter flocks of **lapwing** and **golden plover**. The former group are best seen at around high water on a spring tide: the higher the sea rises the closer to the shore they will have to roost. The concrete embankment to the south-west of the car park is an excellent vantage point and the periodic flights of steps provide somewhere flat to sit and set up a tripod. Meanwhile the section of marsh just on the opposite side of the road may be teeming with fresh water waders and surface-feeding ducks including **pintail** in winter and the occasional **garganey** at migration times. These fields tend to retain water longer than those to the east of the sand winning plant which are at least as rewarding providing they are not too dry. The wettest part of the latter area is the margin along the fenceline quite close to the road. Given suitable conditions the flooded creeks and pools here, besides providing fairly close views of the commoner ducks such as **shoveler** and **teal**, are very attractive to waders. In addition to the ubiquitous **redshanks** and the widespread but well-camouflaged **snipe**, might be found migrant species including **common sandpiper** and even **wood sandpiper** which occurs almost annually here. Some of the waders normally associated with salt water, for instance **dunlin** and **curlew sandpiper**, may also resort to these pools on occasion. When a high tide covers their coastal feeding grounds the fresh water marsh offers a continued feeding opportunity for hungry waders on passage.

Marshside Road, opposite the car park, divides Marshside Marsh into two and can give good views of many birds especially the vast flocks of **pink-footed geese** which may feed in the fields on both sides of this road. These are truly wild geese which breed on the tundra in Iceland and Greenland during the short arctic summer. Among the pinkfeet may be genuine vagrants of species which are much rarer for these parts. However beware the odd escapes, hybrids and feral birds: there is also a permanent flock of feral greylag geese here. Great patience is required to search through thousands of geese on the off-chance of finding a rarity although a **snow goose** for example would be reasonably obvious. The species least conspicuous amongst pinkfeet must be the **bean goose** and a telescope is an essential tool. The differences in the colours and proportions of the bill are not striking and the legs are often out of sight. In addition the apparent leg colour of the pink-footed geese can vary according to the light conditions and to add to the confusion a very few pinkfeet really do have orange legs! One strategy is to look first for orange legs and then carefully study the other features on any such birds. As **white-fronted geese** likewise have orange legs this approach is equally valid on their account. Other rarities do visit this area, for instance there were two juvenile **spoonbills** on the beach one autumn.

2

Headlands and Shoreline

The coastal sites in this chapter obviously include intertidal areas where waders, considered in the previous chapter, are among the typical birds. Away from the river estuaries, the coastline is sandy rather than muddy and this favours sanderling in particular, although many species may be seen especially at migration times. The bird habitats under the present heading, however, are the coastal waters visible from the land and the regions immediately inland from the intertidal zone.

The coastline of Lancashire is devoid of the tall cliffs which make some other parts of Britain such important places for colonies of nesting seabirds. Likewise, although Lancashire has some small areas of stony shoreline from Morecambe to Cleveleys, these are not large enough to support the breeding bird communities typical of extensive shingle habitats elsewhere in Britain.

There are comprehensive sand dune systems south-west of Southport but only remnants of dunes are left between Blackpool and St Annes, since much more building has taken place on the Fylde coast. Dunes nearer the sea are mobile and less suitable as breeding habitat than the more stable ones further inland, which tend to develop a scrub vegetation. The typical breeding species of the dune scrub include linnet, yellowhammer, dunnock and whitethroat while snipe are associated with dune slacks (depressions where water accumulates). Such coastal habitats were formerly the stronghold of stonechats in Lancashire but they are much reduced in number in recent years.

The principal interest of the places covered by this chapter lies not in the breeding birds but rather the passage migrants, and also birds on the sea in winter. Autumn is the most exciting period, when almost anything can turn up. The sea is a daunting barrier to land birds: if they are to cross it they must do so in one flight. On main migration routes birds tend to accumulate on the last promontory of land before the sea, waiting for favourable conditions or sufficient impetus to cross. On the other side, any prominent piece of coastline may represent first landfall for a migrant after an exhausting sea crossing. Many locations on the south and east coasts are famous for this phenomenon and, while Lancashire does not come into this category, any headland will attract migrants to some extent, especially

Preferring more rocky coastlines purple sandpipers are quite scarce in Lancashire but favoured localities include Rossall and Heysham. (B. Marsh.)

inexperienced juvenile birds in autumn. In addition some birds make their way along the coastline for considerable distances. Under certain weather conditions, 'falls' of common migrants occur in suitable places. Birders then search avidly for a rarity which might be amongst them. Tired or disoriented migrants may sometimes be found in unlikely habitat but they tend to choose the nearest thing available which remotely resembles something familiar to them. This will clearly vary between species but may include the beach, a sea wall (possibly sheltering behind it in rough weather), scrub or fields. Wheatears are perhaps the most characteristic passerine migrants to frequent all kinds of coastal locations, although there are many more widespread species, for example skylark and meadow pipit, which are less obtrusive and so easily overlooked as migrants.

In winter the best variety of birds on the shore tends to be around the stony sections and the few outcrops of low-lying rocks. Typical waders of such places are the common species such as oystercatcher, redshank, curlew and knot, plus turnstone and the occasional purple sandpiper which are both specialists of rocky shores. Gulls are also much in evidence all around our coasts. Individual gulls and waders are often very faithful to particular wintering sites, returning year after year. This is usually noticed by the average birdwatcher only when the bird concerned is a rarity such as a glaucous gull. The passerine species to be found on the coast in winter include skylark and meadow pipit again, with greenfinch, linnet, reed bunting and, of especial interest, the scarce snow bunting and twite, the latter often associating with a flock of linnets.

Offshore in winter, ducks and other birds may gather on the sea, often dependent on the state of the tide. Whilst northern England is relatively poor in this respect, both for numbers of birds and diversity of species, commonly seen are cormorant, red-breasted merganser, eider and common scoter. Cormorants and mergansers may often be seen in small groups but eiders and scoters tend to form large flocks. Common scoters breed on freshwater lakes in the arctic tundra but in winter are almost exclusively marine, feeding mainly on molluscs in water usually of five to fifteen metres in depth. In response to the availability of this food supply, their chosen wintering areas may vary between successive years. Great crested grebes frequent coastal waters outside the breeding season as do goldeneye to some extent. Perhaps surprisingly, ducks such as wigeon, usually associated with fresh water, are sometimes seen on the sea. Red-throated divers are occasional while long-tailed ducks and velvet scoters are rarities for these parts.

This chapter could not be considered complete without a mention of seawatching although it is a complex subject and a full discussion is outside the scope of this book. Seawatching is a very specialized form of birding which entails staring out to sea through telescope or binoculars, but certainly with a mounted telescope readily to hand, scanning particularly for those species of bird which can rarely otherwise be seen from land except by visiting their breeding colonies, which are usually located on remote islands. The main bird groups involved are the shearwaters, petrels and skuas, but the cliff-nesting gannet, shag and auks are commonly encountered near their breeding areas. Among the divers, the relatively common red-throated diver, is the most frequently seen on seawatches. Of course most of the birds seen at sea, such as gulls, will belong to species more easily identified in other circumstances and are virtually ignored in a seawatching context. However, one particularly pelagic gull species, Sabine's gull, is much sought after.

Skuas are the raptors of the sea and, with their pointed wings, their flight is reminiscent of a falcon's in particular. They are extremely agile and obtain much of their food by robbing other seabirds of their catch, after prolonged harassment. Terns are often pursued in this way in spite of their being no mean fliers themselves, which can provide some exciting viewing. Skuas, especially the powerful great skua, are quite capable of killing, for food, the target birds themselves. The word 'bonxie' (from the Shetland Isles) is so expressive a term for such a rapacious predator as the great skua that it has caught on and is now widely used amongst birders. As with many large land birds of prey, however, they are also prodigious scavengers.

The main problem with seawatching is that it is very difficult to guess when to go where for the best results. Since the idea is to see pelagic birds, it follows that headlands offer more potential for them to be close enough to the observer for identification. Generally speaking the further the chosen piece of land juts out into the sea, the better the chances. In common with the other attractions of such sites, the best times of year for seawatching are usually during the spring and autumn migration periods. Once again, though, Lancashire is not ideally suited to this activity and many places on the east or south coasts are far better. The North Sea and the English Channel form a migration route for seabirds around the big land mass of Europe whereas on this side of the country many birds pass between the Western Isles and Ireland or down the west coast of Ireland, leaving fewer to be seen from our shores.

Strong winds, including gales, with an onshore component can sometimes bring the birds closer to the shore although viewing is then impeded by waves obscuring birds on or low over the sea and salt spray obscuring the optics! Holding the viewing apparatus sufficiently steady for observation is also a major problem under such conditions. Suffice it to say that the proponents of seawatching are a dedicated band of birders who often spend many hours at a time in their chosen pursuit. The potential rewards are considerable with a very wide range of species, including some migrant land birds, being possible, but it is likely to be disheartening for the novice. Some find the very unpredictability of seawatching one of its principal attractions but the truth is that for much of the time it is actually boringly predictable: miles of sea, no birds to speak of and feeling very cold!

Plover Scar to Bank End

Location

O.S. Landranger Series sheet 102 (Preston & Blackpool) grid reference SD431530.

Plover Scar is situated on the exit channel of the River Lune into Morecambe Bay. From Cockerham take the A588 north towards Lancaster. Turn down the second road on the left in 2.3km, signposted to Cockerham Sands caravan site. Carry straight on where the road becomes a dead end and turn left after a further 1.9km, again following the sign to the caravan site. Just after reaching the coast, park on the right by the roadside.

Access

Room for several cars to park on the upper shore. The public footpath which runs beside the shore is part of the Lancashire Coastal Way. With Morecambe Bay on the left the path leads to Cockersand Abbey and Plover Scar while in the opposite direction it skirts the caravan site and continues to Bank End Farm.

Facilities

Public conveniences in Cockerham (at the junction of the A588 and the B5272) and at Conder Green (see chapter one).

Habitat

Sandy coastline with a liberal scattering of rock, overlooking a vast area of mainly tidal sandflats; saltmarsh; low-lying fields prone to flooding.

Birds

Any time of year: oystercatcher, little owl, greenfinch, goldfinch, linnet.

Winter visitors: great crested grebe, cormorant, grey heron, brent goose, shelduck, wigeon, teal, pintail, red-breasted merganser, ringed plover, golden plover, grey plover, lapwing, knot, dunlin, black-tailed godwit, curlew, redshank, turnstone, common gull, skylark, meadow pipit, black redstart, twite, snow bunting, reed bunting.

Passage migrants: sanderling, whimbrel, yellow wagtail, wheatear.

The striking head and bill pattern of the ringed plover actually acts as camouflage against a background of stones and shingle. (B. Marsh.)

Plover Scar is the tidal area of rocks just off Cockersand Point which is but a small headland buried within the huge estuary complex of Morecambe Bay. From the suggested car parking spot to Plover Scar the shoreline is among the rockiest anywhere in Lancashire whilst the coast in the opposite direction, to Bank End, reflects the more estuarine nature of the area. This combination in close proximity enhances the variety of the site and in consequence the range of bird species found. For example while **cormorants** and **great crested grebes** may be seen off the headland, any **brent geese** or **pintail** are more likely to be found on the sandbanks and saltmarsh visible from near Bank End Farm. In fact most of the ducks congregate around this end whereas the waders are more scattered along the shoreline until the rising tide concentrates them at roosting points such as Plover Scar. Predictably the rocky shore is favoured by **turnstones** but perhaps more surprising are the seasonal visits by **sanderlings** whose numbers regularly climb into the hundreds on spring passage in May.

With regard to timing, the optimum strategy for the birdwatcher depends on the size of the tide. Plover Scar is used as a high-water roost on tides of between about 8 and 9m but spring tides much higher than this will eventually cover the rocks here entirely, forcing the waders to move on. In these circumstances it is better to visit this section of the coastline well in advance of high water and then to try Bank End where birds may be flushed out of the saltmarsh by the still rising tide. On the highest tides many of the waders take to roosting on the adjacent fields which may also be used for feeding purposes if they are sufficiently wet. This applies especially to those by the approach road where besides **lapwing, curlew, redshank** and **oystercatcher**, which habitually feed in such habitats in the breeding season, may even be found **dunlin** on occasion.

This site is also attractive to those passerine species which are often associated with coastal locations in winter. A respectable flock of **twite** comprising some thirty or so birds can sometimes be found roaming over the region between the parking place and the ruined abbey, their peculiar nasal call distinguishing them at once from **linnets**. Although **black redstarts** are rare in Lancashire, shorelines strewn with boulders or concrete, like the portion opposite the caravan site entrance, seem ideal for them. One November day such a bird did put in an appearance here and to make the occasion even more memorable, a short way along the coast towards the abbey a small party of **snow buntings** was found flitting along the embankment.

Morecambe Promenade

Location

O.S. Landranger Series sheet 97 (Kendal & Morecambe) grid reference SD428643.

The longest stretch of easily accessible coastline at the heart of Morecambe Bay. It is possible to park at most places along the front: for the stone jetty (grid reference above), park on the main road in front of the Midland Hotel and walk behind to the jetty.

Access

The stone jetty itself is currently closed to the public while building works are carried out but is due to reopen in spring '95. Morecambe railway station is just on the opposite side of the road from the Midland Hotel. Aim for about the middle of the tidal cycle, that is around three hours before or after high (or low) water. A telescope is a definite advantage.

Morecambe Promenade provides easy access to a long stretch of shoreline which attracts many feeding waders while diving birds frequent the deeper channels offshore.

Habitat

Sandy coastline with some stony sections; broad river channels within the vast intertidal complex of the bay.

Birds

Any time of year: oystercatcher, shelduck, red-breasted merganser, eider.

Winter visitors: red-throated diver, great crested grebe, cormorant, wigeon, pintail, scaup, long-tailed duck, goldeneye, ringed plover, lapwing, knot, dunlin, curlew, redshank, turnstone, common gull, great black-backed gull.

Passage migrants: black-tailed godwit, skylark, wheatear.

The focus of this site is Morecambe Stone Jetty, but included is the whole stretch of coast from Sandylands to Teal Bay (grid reference SD461659), near Hest Bank, which is especially good for surface-feeding duck, notably **pintail**. When the tide is down, the whole of the foreshore is bristling with a wide range of the more common wader species during the winter months whereas less usual waders, for example **black-tailed godwits**, may occasionally be seen. Being situated such a long way into the bay, Morecambe is not well placed for birds of the open ocean but instead is best known for its diving birds on the sea. The stone jetty is a useful vantage point reaching to the edge of the nearest low-tide channel although many of the same birds may be seen from along the promenade. Respectable winter concentrations of **great crested grebes** can regularly be seen fishing this closest river channel yet there are many more in the main Kent Channel further offshore where numbers peak in the hundreds. Small groups of **red-breasted mergansers** come and go while a few **cormorants** are usually scattered around the area also fishing or perhaps perching on any suitable object standing proud of the sea and holding their wings out to dry. By contrast **goldeneye**, which prey on marine invertebrates such as mussels, are found together in a definite flock. As the tide rises they tend to cease feeding when the water over their fixed food source becomes too deep, but often stay in the locality to roost. Similar behaviour has been noted from the scarce winter visitors and vagrants, for instance **long-tailed duck** and **velvet scoter**, which this site continues to attract occasionally.

Heysham Power Stations

Location

O.S. Landranger Series sheet 102 (Preston & Blackpool) grid reference SD407599.

The largest headland within Morecambe Bay, on a significant migration route for all kinds of birds. Follow the main road (A589) to the port of Heysham around a sharp right-hand corner with traffic lights. Turn left at the next traffic lights into Moneyclose Lane going immediately over a hump-backed bridge. About 300m along here is a track on the right leading to the nature reserve car park. See the notice board just inside the hut for a list of recent bird sightings both on the nature trail (managed by LWT on behalf of Nuclear Electric plc) and along the coast which is usually the main attraction. For this part continue down the lane for 850m then go through the Ocean Edge Caravan Park heading for the power stations. The path to the hide is along the concrete sea wall by the power station buildings.

Access

The car park for the nature trail is open from 9:30am to 6pm or dusk. If driving through the caravan site please be sure to obey the strict 5mph (walking pace) speed limit. Low tide is best for gulls and terns on the outfalls but high tide for roosting waders.

Habitat

Power station outfalls; sandy coast with substantial outcrop of rock; scrubland; polluted marsh. With a bleak coastline utterly dominated by nuclear power stations this site is not visited for its scenic value!

Birds

Any time of year: red-breasted merganser, kestrel, water rail, Mediterranean gull, collared dove, long-tailed tit, goldfinch, linnet, reed bunting.

Breeding season: fulmar, gannet, grasshopper warbler, sedge warbler, reed warbler, lesser whitethroat, whitethroat, willow warbler.

Winter visitors: cormorant, grey heron, shelduck, wigeon, oystercatcher, ringed plover, grey plover, purple sandpiper, dunlin, curlew, redshank, turnstone, little gull, common gull, great black-backed gull, kittiwake, guillemot, black redstart.

Passage migrants: sparrowhawk, whimbrel, great skua, common tern, Arctic tern, black tern, goldcrest.

The nature trail has breeding scrubland species such as **whitethroat** but is best for passerines at migration times, with an observation tower as a viewpoint for visible migration. This phenomenon besides being a worthwhile spectacle can also turn up some rarities. However, for the average birdwatcher, this site is more important for the coastal features.

On the coast the first area of note is the rocks at Red Nab which are used by waders and gulls largely as a high-tide roost, this being a likely resting place for a **whimbrel** on migration: nevertheless at other states of tide some waders can be seen feeding here as elsewhere along the shore. These might include an occasional **grey plover**, though they are much scarcer on the northern Lancashire coasts than in the south of our region.

Further along, the wasted heat from the power stations is pumped out into the sea in the form of warmed water at two outfalls. This

A Mediterranean gull in winter plumage might be overlooked amongst black-headed gulls but notice the more prominent bill and white wing tips in the adult bird.
(B. Marsh.)

enriches the food supply in these areas and is the principal attraction for the seabirds, mainly gulls and terns. These focal points are most productive at low tide and can be completely useless at high tide when the outfalls are under water. The first outfall on the route is the larger and is known as stage two (since it relates to the second power station to be built here): it is overlooked by a basic hide. Dainty **little gulls**, a speciality of this site, are regular in autumn and one or two usually linger into winter, while **kittiwakes** are often present after the breeding season and through winter in variable numbers depending on the recent severity of the weather at sea. Heysham is also well known for **Mediterranean gulls** which are fairly regular visitors. The passage of terns especially in autumn can be exciting and may include the odd **black tern**, perhaps a juvenile, any time from mid August to September or even October. Sometimes the terns obligingly line up on the railings by the stage two outfall for easier identification.

While its situation deep inside Morecambe Bay no doubt detracts from its seawatching potential, dedicated observers have seen many scarce seabirds from this site. Most of the birds however are way out into the bay, perhaps even near its mouth, which makes identification impossible except for the very experienced. On the other hand, storms may cause some birds to seek the shelter of the bay and it is then that closer views might be obtained. Storm-driven seabirds are probably best looked for at high tide but under these conditions an appreciable amount of the sea may enter the hide! My most valued sighting here is of my first **little auk** (and still my closest view of this species yet) one New Year's Eve.

Heysham is a good area for wintering **purple sandpipers** which are often associated with the old wooden jetty beyond the far outfall (stage one). Although the jetty itself is in too dangerous a condition for access, one of these birds might occasionally be visible from the shore, roosting on the structure at high tide or feeding among the rocks around low water. Heysham harbour is only just beyond this point but in order to view it and the shoreline opposite, it is necessary to approach from the other side.

Starr Gate and St Anne's Beach

Location

O.S. Landranger Series sheet 102 (Preston & Blackpool).

On the southern edge of Blackpool, this site is the most westerly stretch of the Fylde coast and includes two aspects: the high-tide roost on the beach and the seawatching possibilities.

St Anne's Beach: grid reference SD309307: Approaching Blackpool on the A584 coast road from St Anne's, it is possible to park for the beach just past the Thursby Nursing Home on the left.

Starr Gate: grid reference SD303319: For seawatching continue towards Blackpool and park as soon as restrictions allow after the start of the tramway.

Access

At least for the seawatching location, Starr Gate tramway terminus is very convenient for anyone travelling from the Fleetwood direction while Squires Gate railway station is only about 500m away. A big high tide is usually best for seawatching when it would probably pay to visit the beach first, on the rising tide. Bear in mind that access to the promenade may be dangerous in onshore gales at around high water, potentially some of the very best seawatching conditions, so some discretion is called for.

Habitat

Sandy coastline with some remnant dune systems including slacks.

Birds

Any time of year: kestrel, lapwing, skylark, meadow pipit, linnet, reed bunting.

Breeding season: Manx shearwater, gannet.

Winter visitors: great crested grebe, common scoter, oystercatcher,
                        ringed plover, grey plover, knot, sanderling, dunlin,
                        bar-tailed godwit, turnstone, common gull, great
                        black-backed gull, kittiwake, guillemot.

Passage migrants: red-throated diver, Leach's petrel, Arctic skua,
                        great skua, little gull, Sandwich tern, common
                        tern, little tern, whinchat, wheatear.

At St Anne's beach walk through the dunes and look on the tideline for
the birds which are usually some way to the south. They are inevitably
subject to considerable casual disturbance at such a popular location,
especially in late summer. In addition to **gulls** and a good variety of
waders, terns may join the roost at migration times and I even saw a
party of **brent geese** land briefly on the shoreline. In winter the sheer
numbers of waders in the wheeling flocks are impressive. On the opposite
side of the road the best remaining example of a complete dune system
on the Fylde coastline has been preserved as Lytham St Anne's Nature
Reserve. It is important mainly for the special plants it supports rather
than for birds but **kestrels** are regular and it is worth a look for passage
migrants which may include **wheatears** and **whinchats**.

If the conditions are promising for seawatching, some shelter from
the worst of the weather is very welcome and there are shelters conveniently situated at intervals all along the stretch of promenade suggested. The very end shelter, at Starr Gate, is the one traditionally
used by birders but any of the others provides an equally good alternative (if for example in late summer the noise from the nearby go-cart
track becomes too irritating!). There may be a swarm of gulls visible
by the sewage outfall further along the coast towards Blackpool and
a little way out to sea but the main interest lies in the birds which fly
past or occasionally alight on the sea. **Common scoters** are frequently
seen and sometimes gather offshore in their hundreds although the
numbers tend to tail off towards the middle of the year and none are
likely to be seen in June. Meanwhile **gannets** are supposedly summer
migrants but most years a very few are so late that this species could be
encountered at almost any time except perhaps January. Migration times
are always the most exciting and offer the best variety of birds. For
instance while **divers** are possible in winter, the majority are seen
here on passage. The various species of tern are also migrants but
are more frequent in autumn than in spring and the same applies
to an even greater extent to the **skuas** which pursue them. As with
many of the seabirds mentioned already, **kittiwakes** especially are
more likely to be seen during and after storms at sea.

Formby Point and Raven Meols Hills

Location

O.S. Landranger Series sheet 108 (Liverpool) grid reference SD275065.

Although lying just outside the current political boundary of Lancashire, this headland logically belongs with the rest of the county south of the Ribble. In Formby head for Formby railway station and continue on the other side of the line towards the coast. Follow the road for about 1km to a sharp left corner and after 200m turn right along Lifeboat Road. Park in the car park at the end of the road.

Access

Huge car parking areas. General open access but please respect the fences aiming to reduce erosion to this fragile dune system.

Habitat

Rounded headland with a sandy coastline backed by a complete dune system composed of mobile and stable dunes, scrub and a few small slacks; coniferous plantations.

Birds

Any time of year:	cormorant, sparrowhawk, kestrel, oyster-catcher, sanderling, dunlin, great black-backed gull, stock dove, tawny owl, great spotted woodpecker, skylark, redpoll.
Breeding season:	fulmar, gannet, whitethroat, willow warbler, linnet, yellowhammer.
Winter visitors:	red-throated diver, great crested grebe, common scoter, ringed plover, grey plover, knot, bar-tailed godwit, common gull, greenfinch, goldfinch.
Passage migrants:	curlew sandpiper, curlew, Arctic skua, great skua, Sandwich tern, common tern, little tern, guillemot, meadow pipit, wheatear, chiffchaff, goldcrest.

Although this land projects further into the Irish Sea than any other between the Furness peninsular and the Mersey, it is nevertheless overshadowed by the Wirral and the Welsh coast. Yet in a local context it is a good point for both seawatching and migrant land birds. For seawatching a high tide is virtually essential and a strong onshore wind highly desirable to bring the birds close enough to the coast for identification. If the sea is choppy it may be best to stay on the final ridge of dunes, since from beach level any birds will be hidden behind waves for most of the time. Early one September here I enjoyed my closest ever view of a **great skua**, wheeling along the tideline as it progressed to the south. However it is necessary to arrive well in advance of a high tide to see waders on the beach. The sandy coast is especially attractive to **sanderling** but many other species occur, particularly in the autumn passage period when migrants such as **curlew sandpiper** are a distinct possibility.

In summer the three bird species commonly associated with dry scrubland, namely **whitethroat**, **linnet** and **yellowhammer**, abound in the more stable dunes a little way inland. The dune slacks at this site are not really extensive enough to hold any characteristic birds but are important for the local population of natterjack toads, a nationally endangered species. **Stock doves** are fairly common in the pinewoods and, by local standards, unusually tame and easy to see.

Rossall Point and Area

Location
O.S. Landranger Series sheet 102 (Preston & Blackpool) grid reference SD319480.

This is a headland of some importance at the north-western corner of Fylde plain, marking the southern extremity of Morecambe Bay. Approaching Fleetwood from the south, follow signs to the sea front until the road bends to the right as it approaches the coast. Turn sharp left here instead, and immediately on the right is Princes Way car park.

Access
There is ample free parking on rough ground between the road and the shore. The concrete promenade running along the whole shoreline here is a public footpath. It is best to time your visit to include a good high tide: around 8.5m is barely enough to concentrate the waders. Beware, however, of potentially dangerous conditions when strong onshore winds combine with a big tide to bring the sea onto the promenade.

Rossall Point, one of the stoniest sections of Lancashire shoreline, sees large gatherings of turnstones both feeding and roosting. (B. Marsh.)

Facilities

Public toilets (with disabled facilities) are available back along the main road a short way on the right.

Habitat

Headland on a sandy coastline with much shingle and stones; small lake and pools; golf course and rough grassland.

Birds

Any time of year: kestrel, oystercatcher, ringed plover, lapwing, redshank, turnstone, skylark, linnet.

Winter visitors: red-throated diver, cormorant, eider, long-tailed duck, goldeneye, red-breasted merganser, peregrine, grey plover, knot, sanderling, purple sandpiper, dunlin, black-tailed godwit, bar-tailed godwit, common gull, great black-backed gull, meadow pipit, black redstart, greenfinch, twite, snow bunting.

Passage migrants: sandwich tern, stonechat, wheatear.

From the suggested access point the boating pools and marine lake lie to the east, that is to the right when facing the shore. A walk of about 600m should be far enough to peruse all they have to offer. They often hold **goldeneye** and **red-breasted merganser** in winter and two **long-tailed ducks** overwintered on one occasion. **Finches** frequent the rough grass around the pools or sometimes the shoreline opposite as, very occasionally, may **snow buntings**. The beach also attracts **waders** in variable numbers: in strong westerly winds the bulk of the wader roost may be on this stretch which would afford them slightly more shelter than the traditional roosting site indicated below.

Walking the other way for a similar distance brings one to Rossall Point itself (the next bend past the coastguard lookout). The highest tides are usually the best times to see, outside the breeding season, birds on the sea such as **eider** which sometimes gather offshore in their hundreds. Also at these times waders, including spectacular numbers of **turnstones**, roost close together on the shore between the breakwaters. They are easily overlooked, being so well camou-flaged. This is a fairly reliable place for **purple sandpiper** in winter although it usually requires a diligent search through the wader flock for often only a single bird. At other states of tide some waders may be seen feeding, albeit perhaps further away. Early one spring a **Kentish plover** was present for a few weeks and the following two winters (so far) a bird of the same species, probably the same individual, has been regularly seen. The fringe of the golf course, just behind the sea wall regularly attracts **wheatears** on migration and a **desert wheatear** turned up one November. The strip near the sea wall is also a possible place in winter for small numbers of **snow bunting** or **twite**, the latter perhaps in a mixed flock with **linnets**.

There is another nearby area favoured by **wheatears** and some-times other migrants. This consists of some rough grass fields between Rossall School and the hospital on Westway. Although it is possible to walk to here along the coast, it is more than 2km past Rossall Point and the section in between is not likely to be so good for birds. Hence birdwatchers with their own transport may prefer to make a separate stop here. Parking is available either near the hospital or near the school which is approached from the A587, the main road to Blackpool. The rifle range marked on the O.S. map appears to be disused. **Black redstarts** occasionally favour the area opposite the hospital in winter and rarities on this site have included a **hoopoe** in autumn.

3

River Valleys

The western Pennines attract a high rainfall which gives rise to an immense volume of water flowing predominantly westwards across Lancashire to drain into the Irish Sea, mostly during the autumn and winter. North West Water has identified over a thousand kilometres of rivers in the county excluding their innumerable tributaries on the fellsides. This chapter is concerned primarily with the lower stretches of these rivers and their surrounding habitats. Traditionally these would include the natural floodplains of a river, characterized by meanders, but they are deliberately much drier now through improved drainage and flood alleviation schemes. This has undoubtedly reduced their value to wildlife, in particular for wading birds and wildfowl, however grasslands are still a typical feature of Lancashire river valleys and they can form a useful habitat for a variety of birds. There are often public rights of way along river banks and, besides the birds associated with the river itself, the grassland in conjunction with patches of woodland produces quite a varied and interesting walk. This tapestry of habitats can also, on occasion, make normally inconspicuous birds more visible as they fly between scattered trees or from one area to another: woodpeckers are an example which comes to mind.

Water quality can be important in rivers especially for birds like the dipper whose staple diet is the larvae of aquatic insects. If the water becomes too enriched with excess nutrients, for example by slurry run-off from farms, algal growth can escalate which robs the stream of vital oxygen. Such waters are thus depleted of aquatic insects and the higher forms of life which depend on them. However, if the river is relatively clean and the habitat is suitable in other respects, dippers are able to hold adjoining territories along its length. According to the classification of Lancashire's rivers carried out by the former National Water Council in 1988, almost half their length was of good quality, about a quarter fair and a quarter poor, only five per cent being classified as bad. The Lune was of good water quality for its entire length while most of the other major rivers were good in their upper reaches but became polluted with nutrients, mainly from farming activities, lower down: for example the Wyre was of good quality until St Michael's on Wyre. The Ribble was good

A scene from the valley of the Ribble illustrating the variety of habitats to be found in a typical lowland river valley.

until its confluence with the River Calder which suffers some of the worst pollution of any Lancashire river. In addition to organic enrichment there is metal contamination here, both from mine workings and industrial sources.

Canals are basically similar in structure to rivers in that they form a linear freshwater habitat and, although their waters are more static, would be included in this section. Their value to birds is usually limited by artificial and vertical sides enclosing water of constant depth, however stretches where bankside vegetation and tall emergent plants are well established can prove useful for birds such as sedge warblers and reed buntings. Rivers encompass greater variety in their micro-habitats which is ultimately reflected in the avifauna they attract. Dipper, grey wagtail, sand martin, common sandpiper, oystercatcher and goosander are all characteristic breeding birds of good river habitat in this part of the country. Unfortunately kingfishers are seen much less often, partly because they are so shy: a sudden shrill call is sometimes the first warning that the species is present but by that time the bird is often already flying away.

Reed and sedge warblers, coot, tufted duck, mute swan and little grebe, commonly breed by rivers in the south-east of Britain but are more confined to lakes in Lancashire. Sand martins show an opposite trend, nesting mainly at sand and gravel pits in the south, but using suitable vertical river banks in northern England. They gather where flying insects abound, and hawk up and down the same stretch of river with their buzzing calls which are strangely liquid when heard at close quarters. Like other birds with similar feeding habits, they seem totally oblivious of the presence of people. Oystercatchers are very vocal waders and are easy to locate in flight with their loud, clear piping calls. They will nest on the patches of shingle often left on the inside of meanders, while dippers and grey wagtails frequently use artificial features, such as bridges or weirs, if natural sites are lacking. Pied wagtails can also breed near rivers but may be distinguished even by their call which is not quite so piercing as that of the grey wagtail. Like the wagtails, dippers seem to need some areas of shallow water for feeding and are often seen bobbing on a stone before flying off, with whirring wings and dark rounded appearance, straight and low over the water, sometimes making a deep 'zeez' call.

The grasslands of lower river valleys are generally described by the term neutral grassland. Limestone grasslands have a very restricted distribution in Lancashire and are important mainly for plants and butterflies while acidic grasslands occur mostly at higher altitude on the moorland edge. The neutral grasslands of river valleys usually have poor natural drainage and can remain damp enough to support waders and other birds due to the moderately high rainfall of these parts. Permanent grassland becomes rich in earthworms over the years but if the ground is too dry, birds have no access to these or other invertebrates in the soil. The typical breeding waders of damp grassland habitats are lapwing and curlew with snipe, redshank and oystercatcher in the wetter areas. In a national context Lancashire is an important breeding area for all of these species. Unimproved neutral grassland is rare now in Lancashire as in the rest of the country. The traditional farming methods of moderate grazing and haymaking have increasingly been replaced by silage cropping with the application of fertilizer. These changes have led to reductions in the special birds of this kind of habitat. Hay meadows are the haunt of grey partridge and particularly the corncrake which is now all but extinct in Lancashire.* River valleys are good places to see stock doves which

---

* The RSPB has reported very small numbers of calling males at one site in the county in recent years, according to *Lancashire: a Green Audit: a First State of the Environment Report* (Lancashire County Council, 1991), p. 227.

are more wary than woodpigeons and like to feed with them in the fields but retreat to the safety of the adjacent woodland if danger threatens. This species is rather smaller than the woodpigeon, with a shorter tail and in flight shows a pale central area to the wings contrasting with the dark border.

Scrub is present as an element in so many kinds of habitat but is included in this chapter not because it is particularly more prevalent in river valleys than elsewhere but because scrub in river valleys is arguably the most typical of scrubland habitats. Scrub is a dynamic habitat and will progress to woodland unless permanently held in check by some external factor such as grazing or artificial cutting (or high wind speeds in the uplands). Grazing pressure is a main limiting agent in river valleys, suppressing the growth of scrub altogether in some places. This is not necessarily by human design, for wildlife such as rabbits may be responsible, indeed the threat from browsing animals is the very reason why scrub vegetation tends to be so thorny. Hawthorn is a common and widespread plant in Lancashire scrubland and hedgerows, and attracts a very diverse insect population while gorse often harbours spiders. Likewise willow, also commonly found in scrubland, supports large numbers of insects and so scrub provides an excellent supply of invertebrate food for birds. In addition many scrubland plants produce berries which provides another source of food for many birds, especially thrushes. In autumn scrub is a particularly important feeding area for birds and its overwhelming attraction for migrants at this season is well known. It also caters well for roosting birds, especially finches and buntings. Hedgerows can be regarded as a kind of linear scrub habitat and thick old hedges containing a wide range of plant species support birds such as whitethroat and lesser whitethroat.

The breeding species of scrubland depend markedly on its state of development. Linnets favour the sparsest scrub while yellowhammers move in rather later and are commonest when the scrub is dense but still open. Chaffinches are typical scrubland birds only when the bushes are tall with a closed canopy but dunnock, whitethroat and willow warbler are characteristic species all through this natural succession. Reed buntings are regular in wet scrub but have spread into some drier areas in recent years. Overall the maximum variety and numbers of birds are to be found in dense scrub: normally greater than those of the mature woodland that would in time replace it.

In winter some of the river birds move away: sand martins and common sandpipers migrate out of the country while oystercatchers join other waders on the coast. Wagtails and especially dippers and goosanders can still be found on rivers in winter and grey herons are also commonly seen. The grasslands attract fieldfares, redwings, rooks, starlings and gulls. Common gulls are often found among the flocks of the more widespread black-headed gulls and may locally outnumber them. They have a soft mewing cry quite unlike the raucous calls of other gulls. Winter flooding is not commonplace but can be a focal point for a wider variety of birds, including waders and wildfowl, when it does occur.

Stonyhurst Area

Location
O.S. Landranger Series sheet 103 (Blackburn & Burnley) grid reference SD705392.

Valleys of the Ribble and Hodder near their confluence. From Whalley take the B6246 north-west which passes under the railway and the A59 trunk road. After another 2.7km this road crosses the Ribble at Great Mitton. Almost 1km further on turn left onto the B6243 towards Hurst Green and Longridge. Park by Lower Hodder Bridge which is after 550m.

Access
Room for a few cars at the bridge as indicated above but if walking the complete circuit described below there are alternative parking possibilities along the B6243 at grid references SD701390 and SD691382 which may be more convenient if approaching from another direction. Access on public footpaths including part of the Ribble Way.

Habitat
Archetypal lowland river valley with meanders, flat grassland plains and patches of woodland including some of ancient semi-natural type.

Birds
Any time of year: grey heron, goosander, lapwing, stock dove, kingfisher, green woodpecker, great spotted woodpecker, lesser spotted woodpecker, grey wagtail, dipper, long-tailed tit, marsh tit, coal tit, nuthatch, jay, tree sparrow, greenfinch, goldfinch.

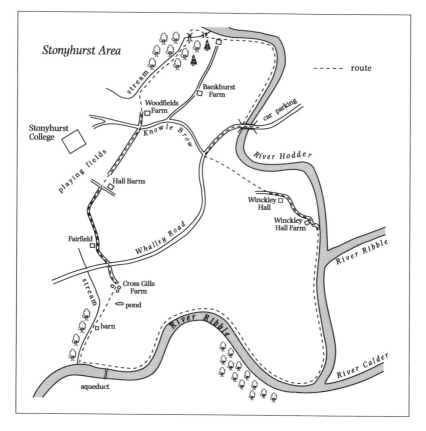

Breeding season: oystercatcher, redshank, sand martin, willow warbler.

Winter visitors: fieldfare.

The trail suggested here includes a walk along stretches of the Hodder and Ribble and links a variety of habitats to form a circular route. It is a reasonably long walk of some 9.5km but involves minimal walking on the main road. Shorter circuits are possible: see the relevant O.S. map. Even from the parking spot at Lower Hodder Bridge a **heron** may be visible on the river bed, patiently waiting for prey to pass by. Cross over the bridge and continue up the road for 450m to a stile on the left almost opposite a side road and bus shelter. Walk along the side of the first field to another stile, then follow the edge of the wood for a while before striking across the field towards a barn. Go through an iron kissing-gate, then another just to the left of the barn.

Turn left onto the track and follow the Ribble Way which is fairly well signposted from this point onwards.

The astute observer may be lucky enough to find **tree sparrows** around the farm, perhaps amongst a flock of house sparrows. The confluence of the Hodder and the Ribble is just as the path comes alongside the river. This is a likely place for sleek **grey wagtails**, catching insects by the water. After another kilometre or so the waters of the Calder, with their artificial nutrient enrichment and cocktail of industrial pollutants, mingle with the Ribble. That the water is of poorer quality downstream from this point is sometimes evidenced by the pervasive odour. Nevertheless **goosanders** are still sometimes found below the Calder confluence. Along this stretch, the strip of woodland on the far side of the river near Brockhall Farm can be good for **woodpeckers** (for closer exploration it is accessible from the other side of the Ribble). On different occasions I have encountered all three species around this region.

Follow the bank of the river until eventually an aqueduct (broad pipeline) crosses it. Shortly after this a band of woodland up a small tributary lies ahead (with a stile and wooden footbridge). Take instead the path to the right following the tributary up the hill: the way is marked with yellow arrows. About half way up near the barn, **stock doves** are usually in evidence giving their simple cooing song in summer. Pass to the left of the barn and also a pond at the top of the hill. There is a stile nearby after which the footpath becomes difficult to discern but head for Cross Gills Farm. The farm track is reached by way of a gate just to the right of the farmhouse. Turn left onto the track to meet the main road and cross straight over. Follow the track to the right in front of a row of cottages and then left and alongside the cricket pitch of Stonyhurst College where vast numbers of **pied wagtails**, mainly juveniles, gather in late summer. Although this section of the trail, through Stonyhurst itself, is mainly to join the path along the Hodder, the other main section of interest, there are nevertheless some worthwhile birds to be seen. A variety of arboreal birds frequent the hedgerows and trees while, in addition to the common pied wagtails, there may be **grey wagtails** in the vicinity. Where the track goes left continue straight on and across a field to join another track which leads out to a road.

Again cross straight over and follow the track until an arrow indicates the footpath to the right, over a stile into a field. From the corner of the woodland just ahead continue along the edge to a wooden stile in the fence on your left. Cross the stile and carry on along the top of the wood until steps lead the way down through the larch forest to a wooden footbridge. An increase in the variety of woodland birds should now be noticed, perhaps including the colourful **nuthatch**, as the coniferous trees give way to broad-leaved species. The route soon joins the River Hodder and follows it downstream (to the right) back to Lower Hodder Bridge. This stretch of river is shallow with many protruding boulders which, in conjunction with the high water quality, makes the habitat ideal for **dippers**. They are often seen along here bobbing on a stone before immersing themselves to hunt insect larvae on the stream bed.

Crook o'Lune

Location

O.S. Landranger Series sheet 97 (Kendal & Morecambe) grid reference SD521648.

The Lune Valley some 6km upstream from Lancaster, near Caton. This area is within the Forest of Bowland AONB (Area of Outstanding Natural Beauty) although outside the SSSI (Site of Special Scientific Interest). From Lancaster or junction 34 on the M6, take the A683 towards Kirkby Lonsdale. Just over 3km from the motorway, turn sharp left onto a minor road signposted to Halton and Crook o'Lune picnic site (brown tourists' sign). The car park is on the right just after the bridges over the Lune and the disused railway line.

Access

Ample parking including an overflow area for busy times. Public footpaths on either side of the river both up and downstream plus access along the old railway line.

Facilities

Toilets in car park.

Habitat

River of first-class water quality which meets all the EC prescribed standards for supporting salmonid fish except for the levels of nitrite; wet scrub, mainly willow, along part of the river bank; improved and unimproved grassland; patches of woodland including some ancient semi-natural areas such as Burton Wood (SSSI).

Oystercatchers breed in river valleys such as that of the Lune and can often be seen feeding in the surrounding damp fields. (B. Marsh.)

Birds

Any time of year:	grey heron, goosander, kestrel, lapwing, woodcock, stock dove, collared dove, great spotted woodpecker, lesser spotted woodpecker, grey wagtail, dipper, goldcrest, long-tailed tit, marsh tit, coal tit, treecreeper, jay, goldfinch, redpoll.
Breeding season:	shelduck, oystercatcher, curlew, redshank, common sandpiper, sand martin, garden warbler, blackcap, wood warbler, chiffchaff, willow warbler, spotted flycatcher, pied flycatcher.
Winter visitors:	common gull.

Although it is also worth exploring the disused railway line to include at least the Crook itself, the main walk recommended here follows the Lune upstream along the north bank as far as Burton Wood and back. For this descend from the car park to the old railway line and take the well-signposted footpath towards Loyn Bridge. All along the first stretch, the eroded bank on the opposite side of the river provides nesting opportunities for the thriving **sand martin** colony. The Lune is excellent for **goosanders** which are almost invariably to be seen flying up and down or fishing in the river.

The path leads in and out of wooded areas where common woodland birds abound and patches of tangled scrub vegetation provide an ideal summer home for **garden warblers** to pour out their mellifluous song. Although confusable, the song of a **blackcap** is more spirited, shows more structure and often starts hesitantly. The tone is also distinct: sharp and precise like that of a song thrush, whereas the garden warbler's song has a mellow tone more like a blackbird. This site would be a suitable place to compare these two fine songsters especially on a spring morning when all the small birds are at their most active.

After 2km or so along the path there is a wide detour in the course of the river and **oystercatchers** often feed in the damp fields hemmed in by this meander. Up ahead on the left is Burton Wood which contains a great variety of mainly deciduous tree species. This is a nature reserve managed by the LWT and a permit is required for access by non-members. The paths within the wood are also very steep and slippery in places. However nearly all the birds mentioned in the above list, including **spotted flycatchers**, can be seen without it being necessary to enter this particular piece of woodland.

Preston Old Railway Line

Location

O.S. Landranger Series sheet 102 (Preston & Blackpool) grid reference SD537289.

A relatively undeveloped area, just to the south of Preston, in the lower Ribble Valley not far from where it becomes an estuary.

Access

Although this site can be approached from Factory Lane in Penwortham, it is in such conveniently close proximity to Preston that a more usual method of access might be on foot from the town via Avenham Park. The park can be entered from various roads, the ones of likely use to the visitor being Avenham Walk, Ribblesdale Place and East Cliff Road which is handy from the railway station: from Butler Street (the exit with the taxi rank) cross the road and the large car park making for the houses opposite which are at the bottom of East Cliff Road (the grid reference given above refers to this route).

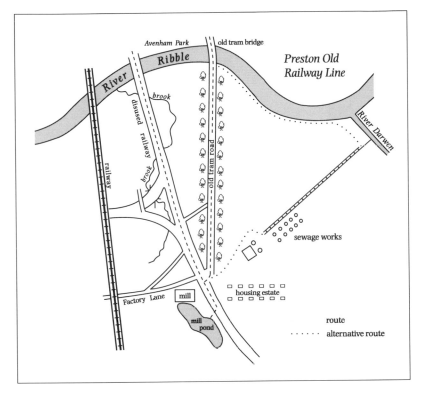

Facilities

Public toilets in Avenham Park just before the disused railway bridge.

Habitat

There is a surprising variety of habitats here within a relatively small area containing elements of parkland, wild gardens, a river with tributaries and muddy banks sometimes exposed at low tide, damp meadows, disused railway embankments, scrubland, a few wooded parts and a disused mill-pond.

Birds

Any time of year: grey heron, goosander, sparrowhawk, kestrel, grey partridge, lapwing, redshank, collared dove, tawny owl, kingfisher, great spotted woodpecker, grey wagtail, goldcrest, coal tit, treecreeper, jay, greenfinch, goldfinch, redpoll, reed bunting.

Breeding season:	great crested grebe, sedge warbler, whitethroat, blackcap, chiffchaff, willow warbler, spotted fly-catcher, linnet.
Winter visitors:	cormorant, snipe, redwing, willow tit.
Passage migrants:	common sandpiper.

Avenham Park supports the expected birds, including **treecreepers** and the occasional hunting **sparrowhawk**, but to reach the main area under consideration go down to the right towards the River Ribble and the bridge which carried the railway line to Bamber Bridge, now disused. This lies between the two other bridges in the vicinity: the old tram bridge and the main railway bridge. There are steps leading up to the path across the bridge which is a good vantage point for seeing birds along the river. **Cormorants** use the Ribble as a flyway and at low tide there is sometimes just enough mud exposed to attract the odd **redshank** or **common sandpiper** on passage.

Following the course of the old railway line, the path crosses and recrosses a small tributary of the Ribble which winds across the way. These points offer a chance of seeing **kingfishers** which have inhabited this brook. Warblers such as **whitethroats** may be seen in the scrub on the embankments or a wandering party of **willow tits** might pause to feed in the taller trees. Where the old line to Southport branches off to the right seems to be a particularly rich area where I once saw a **redstart** on spring migration. A few yards along this track it overlooks the brook again which provides another opportunity to look for a **kingfisher**. **Grey herons** are often seen here as well as on the fields to the left of the main path.

Further on the main path descends to cross a narrow unmade road which links across to the old tram road. Some of the former habitat here has been damaged recently by the 'landscaping' operations when the path was made more organized. However this has helped to deter the unauthorized use of motorbikes along some of the tracks and the section will probably recover after several years' new growth. Just over the unmade road the path joins the other branch from the old Southport line and then it soon meets the old tram road with its long straight avenue of tall trees. These and other mature trees in the area are favoured by **woodpeckers**. There is another public foot-path from this connecting point which leads off over the fields, around a sewage works and along its access road to near where it crosses the River Darwen. One can then turn left and complete the circuit back along the south bank of the Ribble. It was around this area and particularly by the confluence of the two rivers that a **night heron** was seen regularly for a week one spring.

The original path continues and just off on the right is an access to Penwortham Lodge, the water reservoir which used to serve Penwortham Mill. **Great crested grebes** may breed here while the surrounding wet scrub supports **reed bunting** and sometimes **sedge warbler**. Unexpected ducks such as **pochard** or **teal** occasionally turn up on the pool.

Back at Avenham Park, **goosanders** can sometimes be seen from the old tram bridge and it is worth exploring the nearby area around the far eastern corner of the park where it connects with Frenchwood Recreation Ground. I have seen a family of **spotted flycatchers** near the bottom of the path leading up to Selborne Street and **tawny owls** are resident in this region. On the way up to Avenham Walk via the old steps at the very edge of the park it is possible to see into the old rambling gardens of the houses along Bank Parade: this is a good spot for **blackcaps** and other warblers. At the top, **collared doves** are always in evidence by the houses.

Wyre Valley around Abbeystead

Location

O.S. Landranger Series sheet 102 (Preston & Blackpool) grid reference SD564544.

In the upper reaches of the Wyre Valley this site is just outside the Forest of Bowland SSSI (although, as with the Crook o'Lune, still within the AONB).

Access

Parking space at Abbeystead (near the bridge) for several cars between the Wyre and the minor road leading south to Doeholme Farm. Access along numerous public footpaths.

Habitat

Wooded river valley with mainly deciduous woodland and a small reservoir; grazing land with good views of the surrounding fells. Tranquil, unspoilt area with plenty of opportunity for bird-watching in peace.

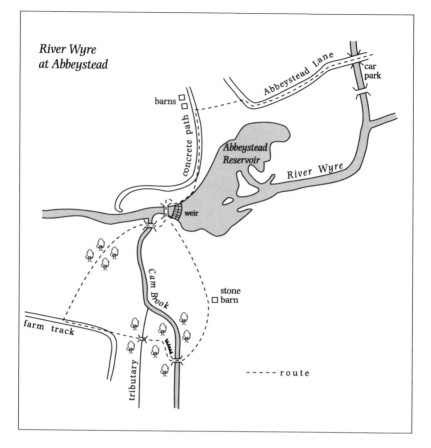

Birds

Any time of year:	little grebe, goosander, sparrowhawk, kestrel, lapwing, woodcock, stock dove, great spotted woodpecker, skylark, grey wagtail, dipper, goldcrest, long-tailed tit, marsh tit, coal tit, treecreeper, jay, goldfinch, redpoll.
Breeding season:	great crested grebe, oystercatcher, curlew, redshank, common sandpiper, cuckoo, redstart, blackcap, chiffchaff, willow warbler, spotted flycatcher, pied flycatcher.
Winter visitors:	tufted duck, fieldfare, redwing, brambling.
Passage migrants:	buzzard.

Good views of **dippers** are virtually assured here if the river bed is thoroughly scanned from each available bridge. The River Wyre is fed by two branches above Abbeystead: the main road bridge crosses the Tarnbrook Wyre while the minor road crosses the Marshaw Wyre on the way to Doeholme Farm. The actual confluence is hidden in the woods nearby. One worthwhile walk involves following the partially wooded valley of the Marshaw Wyre upstream for about 2km and it is towards the end of this stretch where **buzzards** have sometimes been encountered. **Great spotted woodpeckers** are seen quite frequently here due to the relative abundance of dead timber. Take the muddy track almost opposite the car parking area, go through the iron gate and straight along the field to a shed-like construction from where the footpath is marked at intervals by arrows. The hundreds of young pheasants everywhere after their release in autumn can become a bit irritating: most of the strange calls you may hear at this time of year emanate from these birds.

The suggested route in the other direction begins with walking along the road through the village and up the hill. The eastern end of Abbeystead Reservoir is visible from part way up but before the trees start. Near the top of the rise, where the trees finish, there is a stile on the left. Climb over the stile and make for the gate in front of the (leftmost) low barn at the far side of the field. Go through the gate and turn left onto a concrete track which leads down towards the reservoir. It is difficult to see much of the reservoir from the track as it is shielded by trees. As the track bears right there is a marked footpath through a wooden gate to the left which runs a short distance along the bank of the reservoir. Scan the water for **ducks** and **grebes** while waders such as **oystercatchers** and **redshanks** may be found on any tiny protruding islands. A little way downstream from the dam a bridge crosses the Wyre which is a good spot for **dippers** and **grey wagtails**. This bridge is also a good vantage point to look for small woodland birds flitting between the trees on either side of the river.

There is an optional loop from this point of under 2km (but including some steep sections) which is probably best in spring or early summer and encompasses some of the most suitable habitat for **redstarts** and **pied flycatchers**. After crossing the river turn right to cross another bridge over a tributary. From here head uphill through the gap between two fenced-off areas of woodland. Just beyond the left-hand wooded area go through a gate leading to the next field. Up now on the gently sloping valley edge, **curlews** mark out their territories in springtime, resembling miniature versions of Concorde as they glide down pouring forth their evocative song. A few old gnarled trees in a line are all that remain of long since abandoned hedgerows around this area. Follow the old hedgeline in this field and turn left at the end onto a track. After only a little distance the track bears right but keep straight on along a field boundary with the fence on your right. Traverse a stile and narrow bridge, passing through a band of woodland, and go through the gate which is straight across the next field. Hereabouts listen especially for the songs of our summer-visiting woodland birds. Follow the path slightly to the right, down through beech trees, keeping straight on the narrow track which then curves to the right along a small embankment. The footpath follows the wooded tributary upstream to another narrow bridge on the left. Cross the stream and another stile to emerge into a field. The path skirts the woods up on the left and at the top of the rise look to the left for an old stone barn. Go to the left of this barn and continue straight ahead to meet a stone wall. Bear left and follow the wall to a stile at the end. This completes the circuit back to the bridge over the Wyre just below the reservoir.

4

Woodlands

Britain has a paucity of woodland cover compared with Europe: only nine per cent in Britain whereas both Germany and Italy, for example, have around thirty per cent. Lancashire, with a mere five per cent woodland, is sparsely wooded even by national standards. This is in stark contrast to the picture in the past. About five thousand years ago, the vast majority of Lancashire, at all altitudes, would have been covered by trees, mainly of oak (in drier areas), alder (in wetter parts) and hazel. A combination of physical and climatic factors started their decline which was accelerated by the activities of man. Increasing population pressure on the land meant that by the early eighteenth century Lancashire's woodland had dwindled to its minimum level in history. Since then total woodland cover has increased mainly through deliberate planting, initially of a variety of species both native and exotic. More recently planting has been primarily for commercial reasons, especially by the Forestry Commission, and has involved mainly alien coniferous species. Today only about one quarter of the five per cent woodland cover is of ancient semi-natural type, these being the only areas bearing any resemblance to the original wild-wood. Although much of even this woodland has been considerably influenced by human activities, the continuity of these permanently wooded sites, some dating from prehistoric times, generally gives them special ecological significance. The very scarcity of these relic woodlands makes what remnants there are of even more significant value to the kinds of local wildlife which depend on them.

Some species of birds have adapted to the changing habitat: many garden birds are really woodland species which have taken advantage of opportunities provided by people and can often breed at higher densities in gardens than in their natural habitat. The edges of wooded areas often provide suitable locations for species which are typical of scrubland.

Within a given type of habitat, examples which show greater complexity support a greater diversity of bird species. In a woodland context this certainly includes having a good growth of vegetation at each of the various possible levels. This might be achieved by wood-land management techniques such as regular coppicing or by having a variety of appropriate tree species mixed in the wood. Each bird species will then be able to find a niche to satisfy its particular requirements. Related species show these behavioural divergences especially well, emphasizing how they have evolved to coexist in a naturally varied environment without undue competition. For example blue tits feed primarily in the canopy, marsh tits in the shrub layer and great tits on the ground. Blackcaps require tall trees to act as song posts in their breeding territories; garden warblers need dense vegetation at a lower level; lesser whitethroats prefer tall open scrub; while whitethroats choose areas of low scrub. Birds thus respond more to the structure of a woodland habitat, that is how high and dense the trees are and the extent of any shrub layer, than to the actual plant species present. However, these factors can clearly be interrelated, an obvious example being conifer forests which tend to grow tall and exclude so much light from the lower levels that the forest floor is too dark for other plants to survive.

Insects exhibit a much greater degree of affinity for particular species of trees than do birds, some insect species being utterly dependent on a single type of food plant. Trees of native species hence tend to support a wider variety of insects than those of introduced species since the insects have evolved their survival strategies alongside the indigenous trees. Conifers are mostly of species alien to the region and show this reduced abundance of insect life. This may also relate to their smaller foliage area compared with broad-leaved trees, which restricts the available habitat for insects. Thus native and broad-leaved trees generally provide a more plentiful food supply for many woodland birds, particularly the summer visitors which are mostly insect specialists. Coniferous forests may hold other disadvantages for birds: for example the great tit has evolved a breeding season timed to the availability of food in deciduous woodland and seems unable to adapt so well to a coniferous environment. The other main shortcoming of conifers as far as birds are concerned is the lack of natural nest sites, although this can to some extent be counteracted by the provision of nest boxes of various sorts. In Lancashire the largest areas of forest now standing are conifer plantations of relatively recent origin, the most extensive being Gisburn Forest. These are generally located on the higher ground and indeed Gisburn Forest is included under the upland sites in this book.

Alien conifer forests can never be a complete replacement for good semi-natural woodland of mixed native tree species with plenty of old trees. A mature oak tree in particular is a marvellous haven for wildlife with its wealth of feeding opportunities and potential nest sites. In its natural state a wood will have much dead and decaying timber, which is vital to woodpeckers both for excavating nest holes and for feeding on wood-boring insects. Typically there will also be a healthy understorey of sapling trees and shrubs. Many small songbirds commonly feed on this layer of vegetation, and rely on it for nesting, brambles especially being favoured by warblers. There is a notable exception in the wood warbler, a ground-nesting species which feeds in the canopy and selects woodland with little or no undergrowth as its preferred breeding habitat. Abandoned coppice which has grown into high forest satisfies this requirement and, with its now old trees, is also suitable for redstarts and pied flycatchers, both of which nest in holes in trees. Pied flycatchers tend to nest in loose colonies and take particularly readily to nest boxes as an alternative to their natural nest sites. The traditional habitat of spotted flycatchers is woodland clearings but they will use parkland and large mature gardens as a substitute. They like to perch near an open area where they make their aerial sallies after flying insects and thus may be seen near the edges of woodland and along tracks and rides. Their presence is often revealed by their abrupt 'zeek' calls.

Within Lancashire, it is in the Silverdale area where these more natural woodlands are most manifest. They are absent from the Fylde plain and rare in the analogous flat area of intensive farming to the south of the Ribble. In other places the remnants are mainly confined to the steeper slopes in river valleys, which tend to occur on the outside bends of meanders and on tributaries just above their confluence with the main river. The most graphic series of these is along the Ribble Valley from Marles Wood, upstream from Ribchester Bridge, down to Red Scar, near Preston. Some semi-natural woodlands have been altered in character by invasive alien trees and shrubs, most conspicuously sycamore and rhododendron: the latter has often been deliberately introduced for pheasant cover, particularly in West Lancashire. Sycamore has also been planted in the past and the mature trees cast a dense shade, inhibiting undergrowth: grazing pressure in some areas has a similar consequence. This can have an adverse effect on the many birds which use the shrub layer for nesting and feeding, such as blackcaps and garden warblers.

Early morning is always the time of day when woodland birds are most active and easily seen, and in spring all the male birds holding, or trying to establish, a territory will be in full song. In late spring, when all the summer visitors have arrived, the ability to recognize songs really shows its worth, but with everything singing at once it can be very confusing for the beginner. Perhaps it is best to start in March and become familiar with the songs of our resident species

The most widespread woodpecker in Britain, the great spotted may regularly be seen or heard in many Lancashire woodlands. (S. Craig.)

first: by late March the woods will be echoing to the song of chiffchaffs newly arrived from Africa, but at least this is a very easy song to pick up. Another summer visitor, the shy redstart, is also often first detected by his song and even then can still be frustratingly hard to locate, although well worth the effort with his strikingly handsome plumage. Redstarts usually select a song post fairly high up in a large tree, occasionally at the very top, and the song is rather thin and high pitched, quite delicate and almost buzzing in character: pervasive without being obtrusive. It has a definite form which is easy to recognize, with a distinct pause before the final descending phrase.

The nuthatch is resident all year in our woods but is another pretty bird which can be quite shy in this part of Britain. Again it is often first noticed by the ear rather than the eye: a series of loud ringing 'plink's is most characteristic. The treecreeper is of a similar shape and size but, although not shy, with its cryptic plumage is easily overlooked. As they seek insects hidden in crevices in the bark, they work their way up tree trunks in a spiral, and so are out of sight for half the time, then they flit down to the bottom of a nearby tree to continue their relentless search. However even this species has a distinctive call, once learnt: a shrill but quiet 'shreee' as unobtrusive as the bird itself!

The loud 'blick' call of the great spotted woodpecker is easily learnt, but pursuit of the sound through the wood is a futile tactic. The best views of woodpeckers are obtained by a quiet and stationary observer, preferably seated. The related but surprisingly small lesser spotted woodpecker, although more immune to human presence, is not common anywhere in the county and is notoriously inconspicuous. They range widely, especially in winter, sometimes favouring more open woodland habitats, including parkland. They often feed very high up in trees in the thin, sometimes bare, branches at the top. If a lesser spotted woodpecker calls it is usually then easy to locate: the sound can be recognized as a high-pitched even series of 'pee' calls, not ringing in tone as is a rather similar trill from a nuthatch. Tapping sounds can be indicative of a woodpecker although these often turn out to be from a great or other tit hammering away at a nut or similar food item which it has wedged in a crevice.

The raucous conversational calls of jays are easily distinguished but again patience is often required to see more than a shape flying away through the canopy: they are much less tame here than in some parts of southern England. In the autumn they can sometimes be watched flying back and forth engaged in that well-known activity of gathering and burying acorns as an insurance against possible hard times ahead. In winter, a flock of finches suddenly encountered feeding on the forest floor, especially among fallen beech mast, will consist mostly of chaffinches, but it is worth checking for the odd brambling from Scandinavia which may have joined the flock.

Spiby's Wood and Brock Valley

Location

O.S. Landranger Series sheet 102 (Preston & Blackpool) grid reference SD556441.

Easiest to find with a map, but from Inglewhite take Stanalee Lane northwards. After about 2km turn right at the 'T' junction into Bleasdale Road. Continue past the left turn signposted to Brockmill for another 650m, where the road turns sharply right. Take the cul-de-sac straight on at this point. Ignore the right fork to Woodtop Farm and, after a

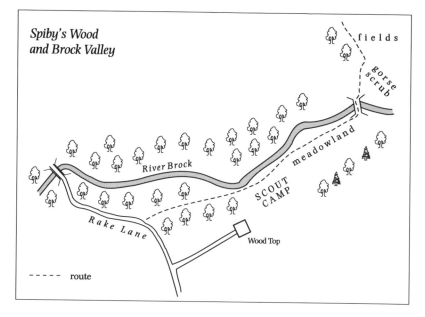

similar distance along the road again, there is a gate on the right
with a sign indicating the public path which is the start of this trail.

Access

Free access at all times on public paths. Can become very muddy
depending on rainfall. Very limited parking space (two or three cars
only) just past the path by the right-hand side of the single-track
road, and further limited space at the end of the metalled section of
the road. There is a scout camp (Waddecar) on the trail which is thus
best avoided at weekends in the school holidays and at bank holidays.

Habitat

Wooded river valley with surrounding grazing land. Mostly semi-
natural broad-leaved woodland but with a small area of coniferous
plantation which adds variety to the whole habitat. The section used
for this trail is not by any means the only stretch worthy of a visit
but is less well known than the Brockmill/Brock Bottoms area and
consequently quieter except when the scout camp is in full swing.

Birds

Any time of year: sparrowhawk, woodcock, stock dove, tawny owl,
                      green woodpecker, great spotted woodpecker,

grey wagtail, dipper, goldcrest, marsh tit, coal tit, nuthatch, treecreeper, jay, goldfinch, redpoll.

Breeding season: oystercatcher, curlew, redstart, garden warbler, blackcap, chiffchaff, willow warbler, pied flycatcher, linnet.

Winter visitors: fieldfare, redwing.

From the gate, the path descends to the plateau by the river and follows the valley upstream (to the right). Many of the woodland birds may be seen in this area including **great spotted woodpecker**. In spring, this whole area is one magnificent carpet of bluebells.

The route continues through the wood and then by the river as it passes the scout camp. Soon it crosses a small tributary and a little further on is a steep bank to the right with tall trees, where there are now nestboxes. A path with steps leads up through this area to Woodtop Farm. **Pied flycatchers** have been present during some summers, especially in this region, but probably do not breed regularly.

The path continues by the river to a stile which leads to a meadow beyond. The small area of conifers to the right of the meadow holds the usual **coal tits** and **goldcrests** and is a possible area for **redpolls**.

At the far end of the meadow is a narrow wooden footbridge over one of the river's two feeder streams. This is an excellent place to scan the rivers for **dippers** and **wagtails**. Being more open, but with woods all around, it is also a good spot to wait for a **woodcock** on his territorial roding flight at dawn or dusk in spring and early summer.

Beyond the bridge the path climbs the opposite bank to the edge of the fields. One New Year's day I watched a **peregrine** from here, soaring and gliding towards me from the fells beyond. Although the path goes through to the road at Bleasdale, it is perhaps less interesting for birds from here onwards. Hence it may be best to return at this point, by the same route.

Back at the gate, the road itself may be worth exploring. At the end of the metalled section a track descends steeply to cross the river further downstream at a fording point. There is a bridge here as well and the path leads up the other side to more fields beyond. **Oystercatchers** and **curlews** are sometimes seen hereabouts since they nest on the surrounding fields.

Mason's Wood

Location

O.S. Landranger Series sheet 102 (Preston & Blackpool) grid reference SD542332.

A small but useful remnant of woodland on the outskirts of Fulwood near Preston. Take the A6 north out of Preston towards Garstang but 1km after crossing Blackpool Road (traffic lights at the corner of Moor Park, with dual carriageway to the left) turn off to the right along St Vincent's Road. At the end of this road turn left onto Sharoe Green Lane and then first right into Sherwood Way. After 600m park in the car park on the left just before The Sherwood pub.

Access

There are many entrances to the wood from the road and the various residential cul-de-sacs. From the car park the nearest way in is just to the right of the complex of buildings opposite.

Habitat

Mixed woodland with brooks, grassy areas and gardens.

Birds

Any time of year: sparrowhawk, kestrel, collared dove, grey wagtail, long-tailed tit, coal tit, treecreeper, jay, greenfinch, goldfinch, bullfinch.

Breeding season: blackcap, chiffchaff, willow warbler.

Winter visitors: fieldfare, redwing, goldcrest, brambling, siskin, redpoll.

This strip of woodland, sandwiched between a golf course and a housing estate, has some more manicured areas around the edges near the houses and these parts tend to be at least as good for birds as the rest of the wood. Also the lower half of the wood (to the right as you enter) seems more productive than the top part.

Mason's Wood is a fairly reliable spot for **jay** and **bullfinch** throughout the year. Both species are often first noticed by their respective calls but the soft piping notes of bullfinches could hardly differ more from the harsh raucous cries of jays. About all they do have in common is being both colourful birds with a white rump, a characteristic coincidentally shared by another species to favour this wood, namely the **brambling**. Bramblings are winter visitors from Scandinavia whose abundance west of the Pennine chain varies greatly from year to year depending on the weather and the availability of food. One winter there was a flock of thirty or more present but the odd one or two are often to be found amongst a group of chaffinches, these two species being closely related. A good strategy is to look first for the largest chaffinch flock in the area and then to watch patiently until every bird has been checked. In a similar way **siskins** and **redpolls** roam in a mixed flock around the wood in winter.

White Coppice to Brinscall

Location

O.S. Landranger Series sheet 109 (Manchester & surrounding area) grid reference SD618191 but the trail continues onto sheet 103 (Blackburn & Burnley) or sheet 102 (Preston & Blackpool).

From the M61 at junction 8 take the A674 towards Blackburn for 1.8km and then turn off right to Heapey. Follow this minor road to the Railway pub (another 1.8km) and there turn left to White Coppice. Continue through the village and up the lane straight ahead towards the cricket ground.

Access

There is plenty of room to park along this lane from where access is on public footpaths or into part of the West Pennine Moors Access Area.

Habitat

Mixed woodland; stream with scrub alongside and a series of pools; moorland.

Birds

Any time of year:	little grebe, woodcock, tawny owl, great spotted woodpecker, skylark, grey wagtail, dipper, goldcrest, long-tailed tit, coal tit, treecreeper, jay, goldfinch, redpoll, bullfinch, yellowhammer.
Breeding season:	great crested grebe, kestrel, curlew, cuckoo, tree pipit, redstart, garden warbler, blackcap, wood

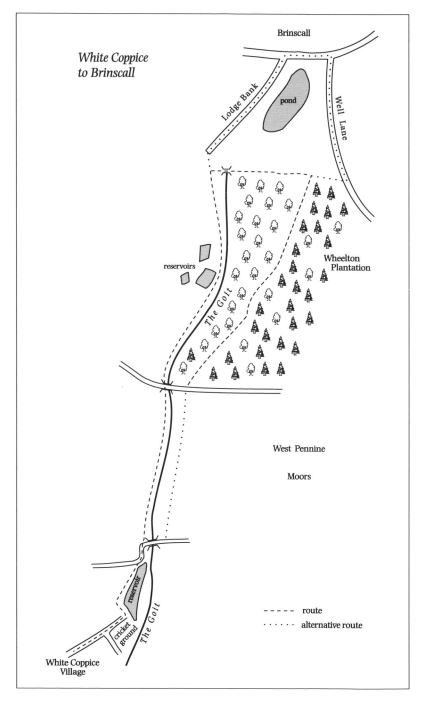

White Coppice
to Brinscall

warbler, willow warbler, spotted flycatcher, linnet, reed bunting.

Winter visitors: common gull, redwing, siskin.

Moorland is dominant to an abnormally low altitude on this exposed western flank of the West Pennine Moors, giving this site an upland flavour and indeed it is quite possible to combine a visit with a walk on Wheelton and Withnell Moors. The West Pennine Moors Access Area begins on the far side of the River Goit: simply walk up the lane, turn right at the cricket field, go past the pavilion, over the Goit and continue onto the moors ahead. Or one can turn right at the bridge to take the path which follows the stream southwards to Anglezarke Reservoir (just over 1km) and cover the Anglezarke site as well (see chapter five).

However the trail intended here follows the Goit northwards to the block of woodland known as Wheelton Plantation. At the top of the lane continue along the track to the left of the cricket field in front of the row of cottages. The path then goes to the left around a mini-reservoir which supports both **great crested** and **little grebes**. After this detour the path joins the bank of the Goit by a bridge. Either continue on the path along the river bank or cross the bridge and use the path on the moorland edge. **Kestrels** hunt the moors and may be seen hovering over the ridge at any point along this route.

Although many species of woodland birds such as **jay**, **bullfinch**, **garden warbler**, or **redstart** may have been seen already in the trees and bushes by the streamside, the woods proper start on the right of the Goit by another bridge. This is Wheelton Plantation which sustains a healthy population of **wood warblers** in the breeding season. They choose the parts with the least undergrowth: stands of mature beech trees seem ideal for them but well-spaced conifers are also suitable. Just on the left as you enter the wood is one favourite spot. In spring immediate attention is drawn to their presence by the plaintive piping notes and quivering trill of their alternative songs. The edge of the woodland can also be a good place to see **goldcrests** especially in winter when their numbers are swelled by continental migrants. These tiny birds are very active, deftly flitting amongst the dense coniferous foliage in their relentless search for insects.

The return journey can be made on the other side of the Goit by taking a small path off down to the left to arrive at another bridge or continuing on the main track through the woods to meet a quiet lane. Descend from here into Brinscall, turn left, go around the pond there and along the residential road which leads back to the same bridge.

Roddlesworth

Location

O.S. Landranger Series sheet 103 (Blackburn & Burnley) grid reference SD665215.

From Blackburn take the A666 south towards Bolton. Turn off to the right on the A6062 signposted to Chorley but shortly turn left again by the Brown Cow pub onto Heys Lane. After passing through the village of Tockholes the car park is on the left just after the Royal Arms pub.

Access

Ample parking space in the car park at the back of the one for the pub. Nature trail and many other public and concessionary paths.

Facilities

Chemical toilets; information centre with limited opening during the summer only. The Royal Arms pub.

Habitat

For Lancashire this is a substantial area of forest, much of it artificially planted but with some semi-natural parts. A very diverse array of trees with a small river, reservoirs and surrounding moorland.

Birds

Any time of year: sparrowhawk, woodcock, tawny owl, kingfisher, green woodpecker, great spotted woodpecker, lesser spotted woodpecker, grey wagtail, dipper, goldcrest, long-tailed tit, coal tit, treecreeper, jay, goldfinch, siskin, redpoll, bullfinch.

Breeding season: great crested grebe, kestrel, lapwing, curlew, common sandpiper, cuckoo, tree pipit, grasshopper warbler, garden warbler, blackcap, wood warbler, chiffchaff, willow warbler, spotted flycatcher, pied flycatcher.

Winter visitors: grey heron, tufted duck, goldeneye, goosander, common gull, fieldfare, redwing.

There are many paths in the core area so I suggest starting with the nature trail and branching out from there. This is a good site for

With its bustling activity and its tail longer than its tiny body, the sheer elegance of the long-tailed tit never fails to delight. (S. Craig.)

exploration since it is not necessary everywhere to keep strictly to the paths (but please keep out of marked conservation areas). In winter woodland birds tend to be concentrated into a few wide-ranging flocks so do not be disheartened if you cover several hundred yards hardly seeing a single bird. It would be quite possible to spend all day in these woods, which extend some 3km south from Abbey Village on the northern edge, but after a while the same species keep cropping up. Wintering **fieldfares** and **redwings** are usually found around the edges of the forest on or near the open fields with their more suitable feeding possibilities. Although the reservoirs are generally rather disappointing it is always worth keeping a look out for the possible flash of a **kingfisher**, while on the connecting river a **dipper** or **grey wagtail** may be seen.

In the breeding season the more open parts with scattered song posts hold a regionally significant population of **tree pipits** and with their prominent, enthusiastic song the territorial males are easy to find in springtime. **Wood warbler** and **spotted flycatcher** can often be located in the vicinity of the bridge where a rough track crosses the River Roddlesworth (paths seem to radiate in all directions from this point). Small numbers of **pied flycatchers** also breed regularly but, although parts of the habitat look eminently suitable, I have yet to find any myself. **Curlews** and **lapwings** breed on the surrounding moors where **kestrels** can regularly be seen hovering in their endless search for small rodents.

Silverdale Area Woodlands

Location

O.S. Landranger Series sheet 97 (Kendal & Morecambe).

In close proximity to Leighton Moss (see chapter five) in the far north of the county within a designated AONB (Area of Outstanding Natural Beauty). Two specific areas are highlighted here although there are many other delightful parts to explore.

Woodwell: grid reference SD464742: Refer to the directions for Leighton Moss but turn left at the junction after the railway level crossing and left again in 350m (signposted to Jenny Brown's Point). After nearly 1km there are public footpaths to both sides of the road and one of those on the right leads to Woodwell.

Eaves Wood: grid reference SD472760: Instead of the final right turn to Leighton Moss continue along the road by Silverdale railway station. After 1km the road turns to the left: keep left at the following junction and there is a car park immediately on the right.

Access

Woodwell: There is room for just a few cars to park by the roadside at the point referred to above. There are many well-marked public paths throughout the region.

Habitat

These woods are very significant in a Lancashire context and incorporate a large proportion of ancient semi-natural woodland together with a great variety of tree species, mainly deciduous.

Birds

Any time of year: sparrowhawk, buzzard, woodcock, tawny owl, green woodpecker, great spotted woodpecker, goldcrest, long-tailed tit, marsh tit, coal tit, nuthatch, treecreeper, jay, greenfinch, goldfinch, redpoll, bullfinch, hawfinch.

Breeding season: garden warbler, blackcap, chiffchaff, willow warbler.

Winter visitors: brambling.

From the birdwatcher's point of view the main speciality of these woods is the **hawfinch**. These birds are very elusive due to their quiet nature and secretive behaviour, spending most of their time out of sight in the high treetops. However, they are not always especially shy of people and if you persevere you may be rewarded by some really close views provided you remain quiet. When this happens you will appreciate their many exquisite features besides the impressive beak. Although they are resident, and so theoretically at least are to be found throughout the year, they are best looked for in winter or early spring when most of the trees are laid bare. As with other species of finch they tend to coalesce into flocks in winter but with the limited number of these birds in the area they are more often seen in small groups. Listen for their 'tick' call (more emphatic than a robin's) and look high up for a dumpy form appearing heavy in flight with a relatively short tail.

Woodwell is the favourite spot to see **hawfinches**. From the parking spot take the narrow footpath, signposted to Woodwell, following the low stone wall. It is sometimes possible to see these birds, and perhaps **bramblings** in winter, from here. However there is a better chance of seeing hawfinches by taking the small path which leads roughly north-west from near the seats in the open area by the well. Just as this path approaches a dilapidated stone wall (where it meets the public footpath) there is a small clearing to the right and a good view of several mature, ivy-covered trees which hawfinches seem to favour. Alternatively the narrow road leading from Woodwell through an avenue of houses has provided some spectacularly close sightings of these elusive birds.

Eaves Wood is another haunt of **hawfinches** and here it is perhaps best to concentrate on the area near the garden centre. For this follow the main path leading from the car park until a definite 'T' junction is reached, then turn to the right and continue to the garden centre through a gap in the old stone wall.

Although the Leighton Moss and Morecambe Bay RSPB reserves tend to dominate the birdwatcher's attention in this region, this whole area is of high quality and woodland birds such as **marsh tit, nuthatch, sparrowhawk, great spotted** and **green woodpeckers** may be seen virtually anywhere all the year round, together with all the usual **warblers** in summer. **Marsh tits** are especially common and this provides a good opportunity to become thoroughly familiar with them and their distinctive call. **Lesser spotted woodpeckers** are very scarce in north Lancashire but I have seen one in this area, which perhaps indicates just how good this woodland habitat is.

Mere Sands Wood

Location

O.S. Landranger Series sheet 108 (Liverpool) grid reference SD448159.

Lancashire Wildlife Trust nature reserve and SSSI close to Martin Mere (see chapter six). From Rufford on the A59(T) take the B5246 towards Holmeswood for 1.4km when the vehicular entrance to the reserve is indicated down a rough track on the left.

Access

Pedestrian access along the marked paths at all times. Car park shuts at 5pm. The Tower Hide (Hesketh Hide) is kept locked but LWT members may obtain a key from the information centre.

Facilities

Very basic at present but major improvements are underway to provide a comprehensive visitor centre with toilets. An innovative underwater hide is also proposed.

Habitat

Broad-leaved and coniferous woodland; scrub and heath; open fresh water with islands; wader scrape; surrounding arable land.

Birds

Any time of year: little grebe, great crested grebe, grey heron, shelduck, gadwall, teal, shoveler, pochard, tufted duck, ruddy duck, sparrowhawk, kestrel, grey partridge, lapwing, snipe, stock dove, tawny owl, kingfisher, great spotted woodpecker, lesser spotted woodpecker, grey wagtail, goldcrest, long-tailed tit, willow tit, coal tit, treecreeper, jay, greenfinch, redpoll, bullfinch.

Breeding season: oystercatcher, little ringed plover, common tern, turtle dove, cuckoo, blackcap, chiffchaff, willow warbler, spotted flycatcher.

Winter visitors: pink-footed goose, wigeon, pintail, goldeneye, brambling, siskin.

Passage migrants: ruff, green sandpiper, wood sandpiper.

In the Middle Ages this area was on the shore of the original Martin Mere which explains the derivation of the first part of the name, while the woodland was initially planted by Lord Hesketh in the mid-nineteenth century. Rhododendron was introduced later and is so invasive that drastic management is now necessary to control it. Although this site is classified here under woodlands, the LWT has tried, with a large measure of success, to incorporate as many different habitats as possible within the space available. This even includes elements of both wet and dry heath which are good for plants and insects although the areas involved are probably not large enough to support any characteristic heathland birds. The total area of open water, created after the commercial extraction of sand, actually approaches that of the woods with the result that the reserve is as important for water birds as it is for woodland species. Although the amount of woodland cover is thus limited, and in real terms is quite small, its value is enhanced by its proximity to the grounds of Rufford Hospital which is but a short flight away over the B5246. Together they form one of the largest areas of wooded land remaining in south-west Lancashire which makes Mere Sands Wood fairly significant in a local context. Martin Mere Reserve (see chapter six) is close by, producing considerable movement of water birds between these two sites.

The Lancaster Hide, just beyond the end of the car park, is the best one for seeing waders. The covering of shells on the bank straight ahead provides ideal camouflage for **little ringed plovers**, which regularly breed, and **green sandpipers** seem just as reliable on passage here as at Martin Mere. **Snipe** might be seen at any season probing the muddy margins of the pools while **stock doves** usually breed locally and sometimes give good views from this same hide. There are several hides placed at intervals on the trail around the

Sparrowhawks are often seen only fleetingly but occasionally may perch in the open close enough to allow the fine plumage detail to be appreciated. (B. Marsh.)

main mere which allows viewing from a suitable angle whatever the prevailing light conditions. Unless the water is frozen solid, **little grebes** are often found close to the Marshall Hide. It is worth scanning the agricultural land all around the edges of the reserve for **grey partridges**. As for the woodland birds, **sparrowhawks** are regularly seen although views tend to be brief except when fortunate enough to witness their display flight in spring. Along the paths in the general vicinity of the Tower Hide there is a fair chance of coming across a few **willow tits**. In contrast **lesser spotted woodpeckers** are by no means easy to find, being so much scarcer than the **great spotted** variety and easily overlooked unless alerted by the call, which seems to be given most often in springtime. Mere Sands Wood is also noted as being one of the last strongholds in the region for native red squirrels which are usually found in the coniferous section of the woods.

5

Fresh Water Lakes and Reedbeds

Wetland habitats have been in decline for centuries over much of Europe, mainly at the hands of mankind. Threatened with drainage for agricultural improvement; pollution from farming, industry and waste; leisure development and associated disturbance, their demise has dramatically accelerated in recent decades. Only recently has their full value begun to be widely recognized and effective conservation measures been taken in some areas. The international convention on wetlands which took place at Ramsar, Iran in 1971 may be seen as a turning point in the fortunes of these vulnerable habitats. In Lancashire we are fortunate to have such a fine example of a freshwater wetland area as the RSPB reserve at Leighton Moss which is accordingly designated as a Ramsar site and SPA (Special Protection Area).

The quality of a lake for wildlife depends primarily on the emergent and surrounding vegetation which provides food for birds both directly and by virtue of the insects and other small creatures which it harbours. In their natural state wetlands tend to gradually dry out, although new wetland areas would be formed concurrently as replacements. Initially the edges of the open water are colonized by plants such as reeds then, as the dead growth accumulates, the ground level rises allowing other, less water-tolerant, plants to dominate in the intermediate damp conditions. The process continues with scrub encroachment until finally a climax vegetation is reached which over most of Britain means broad-leaved woodland. At any snapshot in time this succession of vegetation types may be observed in the horizontal plane: the further away from the open water the drier, and slightly higher, the ground, with its corresponding kinds of plants. Habitats where substantial areas of all these stages are present simultaneously support the greatest variety of wildlife from aquatic species to, for example, the song birds of the marginal regions. Active management, such as the cutting and removal of reeds, is needed in order to maintain this snapshot indefinitely at any given wetland site like a nature reserve. By contrast, steep-sided bodies of water with no shallow margins leave little opportunity for encroaching vegetation to become established and are likely to remain relatively unchanged without much interference. Reservoirs are often of this nature and may differ in other ways which will be considered below.

The plants in turn are greatly influenced by the quality of the water. Pure water rarely exists for long in nature: it soon picks up minerals from surrounding rocks and organic nutrients from many sources. So important is the nutrient content of water that it forms a basis for classifying lakes according to their trophic status. The main categories are oligotrophic (low in nutrients) and eutrophic (high in nutrients). Oligotrophic lakes tend to be deeper, more acidic and situated at higher altitude. They are relatively unproductive because the growth of plants is restricted by the lack of nutrients and sometimes by the generally higher wind speeds in the situations where they occur. Windy conditions can mobilize sediment from the bed of a shallow lake making the water more opaque which thus limits the light available to aquatic plants. Deeper lakes suffer from reduced light penetration in the first place. Many Lancashire reservoirs are typically oligotrophic but, being at higher altitudes, their birdlife is discussed in the chapter on uplands.

Eutrophic lakes, on the other hand, generally support greater numbers and a wider range of species of birds, both in the breeding season and as a winter refuge, principally on account of the greater availability of food. Artificial nutrient and organic enrichment, originating from agricultural fertilizer run-off, farm slurry and sewage, occurs widely in the lowlands of Lancashire mainly in association with areas of intensive farming. While in principle a small amount of such pollution might make an oligotrophic lake more productive and hence support a greater variety of birds, too much quickly leads to lower diversity among all forms of life. The excess nutrients encourage rampant growth of algae, cutting out the light needed by other plants, followed by depletion of oxygen in the water as the dead algae decay. This process is termed hypereutrophication and can be fatal for aquatic animals including fish. The concentrations of ponds in Lancashire broadly correlate with the main areas of dairy farming and many are surely polluted to some degree by nutrient run-off from farms. Their small size compared with lakes also limits the number of bird species which can effectively utilize them. Although collectively ponds may be significant for local wildlife, individually they are not in general worth a special visit for birds.

The shape of a lake is important in determining the amount of marginal vegetation possible and lakes with convoluted shorelines are generally better for birds. This applies especially to breeding dabbling

A view from the public hide at Leighton Moss. This site is of national importance for the bitterns and bearded tits which live in its fine reedbed habitat.

ducks which set up feeding territories around the edges of a body of water. The same principle, that increasing the ratio of edge to centre in a habitat is beneficial to most wildlife, holds in much more general circumstances. In particular, bitterns prefer to feed in the margins of reedbeds and so areas of open water within the reeds are important for them as they are for other species such as kingfisher, rails and wildfowl. Islands in large lakes provide not only more shoreline but also some security for nesting and roosting birds from predators. The physical layout of a site can also have an impact on how useful it is to birds. Trees closely surrounding a small lake may make it difficult for heavier birds such as wildfowl to take off and land, as well as concealing potential predators, including people.

The three British bird species most dependent on reedbeds for nesting, bearded tit, bittern and marsh harrier, all breed in Lancashire, notably at Leighton Moss. They are all rare in a national context, their only other main breeding area being the Norfolk Broads and similar habitats nearby. Bearded tits have been on the increase in the latter half of this century and marsh harriers are at least holding their own now, but the continuing decline of the bittern in this country is giving serious cause for concern. In spite of their name reed warblers are not so confined to reedbeds but, in common with the above species, they approach the northern limit of their British range here. That the cause is merely lack of suitable habitat is evidenced by the fact that in each case the species breeds further north in mainland Europe. Reeds are especially useful to birds since they have the required physical strength for supporting nests and acting as song posts which some other kinds of fen vegetation lack. Reedbeds also provide good roosting sites particularly in late summer for species such as sand martin, swallow, starling and various buntings.

Sedge and reed warblers are two closely related species which are often present together but potential competition between them is reduced by behavioural adaptations. These operate both in the vertical and horizontal planes to largely separate the species by preferred habitats. Sedge warblers tend to nest and feed lower down in the vegetation than reed warblers. Reed warblers tend to nest in the reedbed but feed in the surrounding willow woodland while sedge warblers occupy the marshy scrubland in between but show some bias towards feeding in the reedbed.* The reed warbler thus requires a greater disparity of habitat within easy reach which renders sites without the full range of features less attractive to this species for breeding purposes. Sedge warblers, however, are more adaptable and so will be found to be more widespread. Reed warblers generally keep well hidden especially when singing and are thus much harder to see than sedge warblers until autumn when young birds are around and numbers may be swelled by an influx of migrants. Although recognizably similar in overall character, the even, rhythmic song of the reed warbler contrasts with the more spirited, mimetic but often grating song of the sedge warbler.

The transition zone often known as high marsh is normally dominated in summer by sedge warblers and reed buntings which between them typically account for about half the total breeding birds of this region. Reed buntings have a simple but variable song, somewhat buzzing in tone, with a particularly measured delivery. Further out from the marsh, in the carr and scrub, bullfinches and redpolls are typically to be found. Lesser spotted woodpeckers are especially associated with alder carrs where there is much rotting wood from fallen trees due to the unstable ground.

---

* Cited in R. J. Fuller, *Bird Habitats in Britain* (T. & A. D. Poyser, 1982), pp. 155–6.

On the open water itself, wildfowl are generally fairly obvious although garganey may stay hidden in vegetation for long periods. Migrating terns are sometimes seen and in particular black terns hawking insects over a lake, or picking them from the surface, are a special bonus. They are most likely to be found after easterly winds in early May as large numbers of them are migrating north through the continent at around this time. The longer the duration of the easterlies, the further west they tend to drift.

Wayoh Reservoir and Entwistle

Location

O.S. Landranger Series sheet 109 (Manchester & surrounding area) grid reference SD721172.

Not far from Bolton, this area is on the southern edge of the current county of Lancashire and is included in the West Pennine Moors CMA (Countryside Management Area). From Darwen take the A666 towards Bolton and after about 2.5km from the southern edge of the built-up area turn left onto the B6391 for Turton and Turton Tower. After just over a further 2km a wooden sign indicates the access to a car park on the left.

Access

Very handy for rail travel to Entwistle station on the Blackburn to Manchester line. Wayoh Reservoir is a nature reserve managed by the LWT but there is free public access on footpaths.

Facilities

Strawbury Duck Inn.

Habitat

Reservoirs, streams, coniferous, mixed and broad-leaved woodland, carr and rough grassland.

Birds

Any time of year: teal, stock dove, collared dove, green woodpecker, great spotted woodpecker, goldcrest, long-tailed tit, willow tit, coal tit, treecreeper, jay, goldfinch, redpoll.

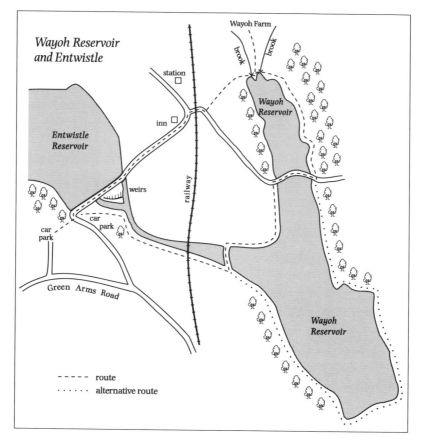

Breeding season: great crested grebe, kestrel, lapwing, common sandpiper, kingfisher, blackcap, chiffchaff, willow warbler.

Late summer: grey heron.

Winter visitors: whooper swan, wigeon, pochard, tufted duck, goldeneye, goosander, redwing, brambling, siskin.

There are many footpaths enabling comprehensive exploration of the region which can be rather confusing at first. A good introduction to the variety the area has to offer can be obtained from a circular walk of some 3.5km and although it is described below starting from the car park, it passes right by the station and so is equally convenient for rail travellers.

From the higher car park referenced in the location details, walk down to the right and cross the larger lower car park by Turton and Entwistle Reservoir. This car park is reached via the minor road which joins the B6391 slightly nearer Chapeltown (and Bolton) and would be the one to use if approaching the site from the south. Turton and Entwistle Reservoir itself should be checked in passing but is often devoid of birds: they favour instead Wayoh Reservoir which held a male **ring-necked duck** during one recent winter.

Follow the woodland trail marked by arrows, keeping the stream and weirs on your left, pass under a railway bridge and continue as the stream widens into one arm of Wayoh Reservoir. Coming out of the wooded area, turn left to cross this stretch of water on a causeway which provides a good vantage point for both water birds and larger woodland species such as **jay** and **woodpeckers**. If you are lucky enough to see **kingfishers** here, the open vista means they may stay in view for longer than is all too often the case. As they fly away the bright blue stripe up the back is most conspicuous making them seem even more like tropical birds out of place. On the far side of the causeway turn right and follow the reservoir around until the path meets a road. Turn right onto the road crossing the second arm of the reservoir on another causeway. Scan the deeper main part of the reservoir to the right for **grebes** or **diving ducks** and larger species such as **swans**. It is quite possible to walk right round this section as well which would almost double the length of the trail.

Turn left from the road into the woods again, following the northern arm of the reservoir which has fairly extensive carr habitat ideal for **willow tits**. In the northern half of Lancashire marsh tits would predominate in such situations while willow tits seem mainly confined to the south of our region. Recently marsh tits in Lancashire appear to have been growing in number and expanding their range southwards. The two species are easily confused, their most obvious difference being the calls which are well documented in the field guides. However there are also more subtle differences: in willow tits the colours tend to merge more giving a softer, diffuse appearance and their behaviour is rather less active making them harder to notice, whereas marsh tits seem characteristically neat, lively and cheeky.

Where the path crosses two streams close together on wooden bridges there is a small path off to the right between them. This leads up to Wayoh Farm and may be worth a short detour for a view from more open land over the woods and to the moors beyond. **Kestrels** sometimes perch on the electricity poles and cables here. After the second bridge take a smaller path on the right, leading diagonally uphill through a small coniferous area, which comes out to a rough grass field. Continue uphill across the field and over a stile to rejoin the road. Turn right and the railway station and Strawbury Duck are at the top of the hill. The track along the left-hand side of the inn leads back to the car parks.

Anglezarke

Location

O.S. Landranger Series sheet 109 (Manchester & surrounding area) grid reference SD620161.

From Chorley take directions south-eastwards for Rivington. The minor road parallels the M61 for about 2km until the Bay Horse pub. Turn left here to cross the motorway and then immediately left again. Just over 1km further on is a causeway separating Anglezarke Reservoir from Rivington Reservoirs, followed by a sharp left turn. Turn left again at the 'T' junction 450m ahead and the entrance to the car park is straight ahead on the very sharp right turn at the bottom of a steep hill.

Access

Ample car parking areas and plenty of public footpaths.

Habitat

Large reservoir which is part of a chain stretching almost 6km; mainly deciduous woodland; moorland.

Birds

Any time of year:	great crested grebe, common scoter, sparrowhawk, kestrel, lapwing, little owl, skylark, meadow pipit, grey wagtail, long-tailed tit, coal tit, nuthatch, treecreeper, jay, goldfinch, yellowhammer.
Breeding season:	oystercatcher, garden warbler, willow warbler, linnet.
Winter visitors:	cormorant, grey heron, wigeon, teal, goldeneye, red-breasted merganser, goosander, common gull, fieldfare, tree sparrow, brambling, siskin.

As at nearby White Coppice (in chapter four), this site is very exposed to prevailing westerlies which brings the transition to moorland much lower than usual. Heather flourishes wherever grazing by sheep is sufficiently controlled. It is difficult to know how to classify a site such as this in terms of habitat, the woodland birds being perhaps as significant as the water-dependent species. The upland appearance of the area only adds to the confusion although one would probably have to walk up onto the moors themselves to see any characteristic upland species such as red grouse.

The footpath leading slightly downhill from the car park soon provides an elevated view over Anglezarke Reservoir but a telescope would be advisable as some of the birds may be quite distant. Continuing around the marked woodland trail, be prepared for **bramblings** in winter. They have a distinctive sharp nasal call with an upwards inflection but are generally silent whilst actually feeding on the ground, usually among the fallen leaf litter with a flock of chaffinches. When disturbed they fly back up to the trees for safety and the surprisingly narrow white rump is not always easily seen unless one should fly directly away from the viewer. There is rarely anything of special interest on the small higher reservoir although it may offer close views of the odd **goldeneye** in winter. At the far corner of this reservoir another footpath leads up to Manor Farm and it is perhaps up here, on the moorland edge, where a **little owl** is most likely to be seen. Given the right spring conditions, the wistful descending cadence of **willow warbler** song fills the young woodland growing up the lower slopes of the hillside here. Most of these birds may be only pausing on migration but some will remain all summer to breed. Continuing along the main reservoir there is a footpath which gives views over the northern section. If the water level is low there may be a few rocks exposed in the middle forming a tiny island which sometimes collects a roosting wader, such as an **oystercatcher**, as well as gulls. From the north end of the reservoir one can cross the road and continue on a path to reach White Coppice (see chapter four) in a little over 1km.

I have not seen any true rarities at this site (although **common scoters** are scarce inland) but the adjacent Rivington Reservoirs have attracted both **red-throated diver** and **red-necked grebe** simultaneously during one winter spell. Upper and Lower Rivington Reservoirs can be best viewed simply from the road causeway dividing the two.

Foulridge Reservoirs

Location

O.S. Landranger Series sheet 103 (Blackburn & Burnley) grid reference SD879419.

Among the most easterly stretches of open water in Lancashire. From Colne take the A56 north towards Skipton, passing between the two reservoirs. Foulridge Upper Reservoir can be viewed from the main road by parking on the side of the minor road at grid reference SD890412. For the lower reservoir, turn left in Foulridge onto the B6251 for Barnoldswick and after 600m bear left again into a minor road at a sharp right-hand corner. Park by the roadside in about another 600m near the ford just past the sailing club buildings.

Access

This suggested parking area can become crowded when there is a fishing match on, for example: there are alternatives back on the housing estate in Foulridge. Good gravel footpath around Foulridge Lower Reservoir to join the main road. There is a hide but it is kept locked due to vandalism (key available from Foulridge Stores, Skipton Road, Foulridge) and it is unlikely that any additional birds would be seen from it.

Habitat

Reservoirs surrounded by scrub and damp meadows; small stream.

Birds

Any time of year: little grebe, lapwing, coal tit, tree sparrow, greenfinch, goldfinch, bullfinch.

Breeding season: great crested grebe, grey wagtail, sedge warbler, willow warbler, linnet, reed bunting.

Winter visitors: cormorant, grey heron, whooper swan, wigeon, pochard, tufted duck, goldeneye, goosander, golden plover, common gull, meadow pipit, fieldfare, redwing.

Passage migrants: common sandpiper, common tern, black tern, sand martin, yellow wagtail, redpoll.

These reservoirs form the easternmost body of water at moderate

A pair of great crested grebes guarding a chick. At this age the chicks will often ride in the safety of their parents' backs. (S. Craig.)

altitude in Lancashire, while their situation in a valley means that they are well placed for both general migration and trans-pennine movements. In consequence there is a relatively good chance of **black terns** on passage as well as other migrants. Fruitful visits are often made in spring at the same time of year as the dotterel frequent Pendle Hill which is conveniently fairly close by (see chapter seven). Although Foulridge can be disappointing I would prefer to describe it as unpredictable with the upper reservoir especially being the sort of place where anything may turn up, for instance there was a **ring-necked duck** one November. Flocks of grazing **wigeon** and impressive numbers of **goosander** are reasonably regular here in winter while hundreds of **lapwing** and **golden plover** sometimes feed on the margins.

It is best to walk right round the lower reservoir to take advantage of the varying angle of the light, even though this entails going along the busy main road for about 500m. If parking where recommended, join the path near the sailing club at the western end of the reservoir, looking for **grey wagtails** by the outlet stream. Sailing activities cause little if any disturbance to the birds since no power craft are involved. The various buoys towards this end of the reservoir make convenient perches for migrant **terns** taking a rest between bouts of fishing or hawking insects over the water and hirundines, including **sand martins**, gather on the overhead wires to the right. **Common sandpipers** fly from the waterside giving their clear high-pitched calls and gliding on stiffly bowed wings, while the numbers of **yellow wagtails** on passage in the adjacent fields often reach double figures with the chance of an individual of a different race amongst them. Early spring witnesses an accumulation of **great crested grebes** and some pairs may breed if water levels are sufficiently high whilst **little grebes** favour the end of the reservoir near the main road where there is thicker cover. In winter there are just a few diving ducks, such as **goldeneye** and **tufted duck**, but more surprisingly so far inland is the frequent occurrence of **cormorants**.

Leighton Moss
and Allen and Eric Morecambe Pools

Location

O.S. Landranger Series sheet 97 (Kendal & Morecambe).

RSPB nature reserves in the northern reaches of the present administrative county of Lancashire.

Leighton Moss: grid reference SD477750: From junction 35 on the M6 turn right at the roundabout to follow the A6 north towards Milnthorpe. In about 1km turn left at a minor crossroads just before the next roundabout. This road leads to Warton where you turn left at the main street through the village. At the far end of the settlement take a right turn on a wide sweeping bend rather than continuing towards Carnforth. (If originally travelling north on the A6, this is the other end of a short-cut from Carnforth). Follow this road for about 4.5km and then turn right (500m after crossing the railway line). The reserve entrance is just down the next road on the right before the station.

Allen and Eric Morecambe Pools: grid reference SD475737: The access track is located on a bend in the road 400m before the railway level crossing if following the directions to Leighton Moss Reserve given above. Along the rough track and under the low railway bridge there is a small car park to the left.

Access

Leighton Moss: Car parking to the front and rear of the reception building although even this large area can become full at peak times. Silverdale railway station is barely 250m distant. Public causeway with hide open at all times; access to the rest of the reserve, with four more hides, entails a charge for non-members of the RSPB (members free). The nearest hide (Lilian's) is particularly suitable for wheelchair access but some others are also accessible (see information at the Centre). Note that the noise from clay pigeon shooting every Sunday morning on Warton Crag carries a long way and can become very irritating.

Facilities

Leighton Moss: Toilets including disabled facilities. Centre opens at 10am with RSPB shop selling books, gifts, etc; information display with television screen showing live images from the bird table and a hide; café.

Habitat

Ramsar site and SPA (Special Protection Area). First-class reedbed habitat, open fresh water of various depths, wader scrape, saltmarsh, scrub and woodland with rough grazing land around.

Birds

Any time of year:	bittern, grey heron, shelduck, teal, shoveler, pochard, tufted duck, kestrel, water rail, oystercatcher, lapwing, dunlin, snipe, curlew, redshank, collared dove, little owl, bearded tit, linnet, yellowhammer, reed bunting.
Breeding season:	garganey, marsh harrier, skylark, whinchat, grasshopper warbler, sedge warbler, reed warbler, lesser whitethroat, whitethroat.
Winter visitors:	greylag goose, wigeon, gadwall, pintail, goldeneye, smew, red-breasted merganser, goosander, hen harrier, peregrine, spotted redshank, common gull, kingfisher, fieldfare, redwing, tree sparrow, siskin.
Passage migrants:	osprey, little stint, curlew sandpiper, ruff, black-tailed godwit, greenshank, wood sandpiper, common sandpiper, little gull, sand martin.

With sixty-seven species of bird regularly breeding, Leighton Moss is a marvellously rich area, of national importance for its reedbed habitat and the **bitterns** and **bearded tits** which this supports (hence its inclusion in this chapter rather than with mosslands). For the sake of clarity, the woodland species have been omitted from the above list but all the species listed under the Silverdale Area Woodlands site (see chapter four) may be found on or around the Leighton Moss Reserve except perhaps hawfinch. For example **green woodpeckers** are often seen, or at least heard, in the fields opposite, when walking along the road from the reception building to the public causeway. However I would refer the reader to a useful book entitled *Walks in the Silverdale/Arnside Area* by R. Brian Evans (Cicerone Press, 1986) and in particular to walk number 3. This circuit joins together Leighton Moss, the Allen Pool complex and a good variety of other habitats in the area including Woodwell which is well known for hawfinches. The route also offers good views from near the foot of Warton Crag over the Leighton Moss Reserve as a whole which has the advantage that if a **harrier**, for example, is flying it will be visible albeit not as closely as from one of the hides.

There is a wealth of information at the Centre embracing which species of birds and mammals are on the reserves and also what unusual birds have been seen recently in the surrounding region including Heysham and Morecambe, Dockacres Gravel Pits and the Kent Estuary at Arnside.

Lilian's Hide is the first one on the path leading from the back of the car park and often produces the closest views of **bitterns** especially when freezing conditions bring them out to the edge of the reeds. Further on, the Grisedale Hide gives access to the very heart of the reedbed and so is usually the best viewpoint for **harriers**. The public hides on the causeway overlook the largest area of open water and are generally best for **diving duck** but also offer a good chance of seeing a **bittern** since a greater length of the reedbed edge is visible. In spring bitterns can regularly be heard giving their territorial booming call which sounds like someone blowing across the mouth of an empty bottle. The dreadful squealing call of **water rails** is also heard much more often than these very shy birds are seen. However one memorable day water rails were behaving more like moorhens: the ground had been frozen solid for some weeks so on the first day of the thaw they were to be seen feeding ravenously very close to the public causeway even at around midday. Another amazing winter's day **bearded tits**, normally so elusive, were equally in abundance although the public causeway at around mid morning often offers a

The cryptic colouration of the bittern enables them to blend in with the reeds and only rarely are they seen out in the open, usually when the water is frozen. (B. Marsh.)

good chance of sightings on calm days. The far hide, reached from along the path to the left at the far end of the causeway, is not so frequented by people and can be another good spot for **bearded tits** and other difficult or shy species. This path around the back of the reserve, not neglecting the section beyond the far hide, includes some of the finest woodland habitat on the reserve. The path eventually rejoins the road where one can turn left and walk back to the reserve entrance, enjoying good views over the northern end of the reserve on the way (the entire loop back to the public causeway covers some 3.5km).

The Allen and Eric Morecambe Pools are actually part of the More-cambe Bay RSPB Reserve but are so close to Leighton Moss that they are usually thought of together. **Whinchats** sometimes breed nearby and are most often seen in late summer when the young are on the wing. The field to the right on the approach to the first hide is delib-erately managed to attract large flocks of **finches** once the breeding season is over and is noted for **tree sparrows** in winter. The pools

are an excellent place for **waders** of which there tend to be more
here when a high tide reduces the available feeding area in Morecambe Bay. The second hide offers more scope as it overlooks both
pools and often the Eric Morecambe Pool holds a greater variety of
birds. However it depends on the water levels, particularly on the
Allen Pool which varies more dramatically sometimes causing the
waders to congregate there. Rarities in this area have included
spoonbill, black-winged stilt and **snow goose** while at Leighton
Moss the impressive list contains **little bittern, Savi's warbler**
(which sang regularly in the early mornings one spring), **ring-
necked duck** and **ferruginous duck**. Besides actual rarities the
habitat is so good that scarce birds will continue to turn up relatively
frequently, previous examples being **pied flycatcher, Arctic tern**
(on passage), **scaup** (in winter) and **Mediterranean gull** which may
even breed in the future.

Dockacres Gravel Pits

Location

O.S. Landranger Series sheet 97 (Kendal & Morecambe) grid reference
SD522723.

From Carnforth take the A6 north, or from junction 35 on the M6 turn
right at the roundabout onto the A6. About 1km north of the roundabout turn right at the crossroads into Borwick Lane. Turn right again
at the crossroads just after the motorway bridge. After about 500m there
is a convenient viewing point from a gateway on the right. Cyclists will
probably prefer to find the minor road running north-east from Carnforth, turn left at the end, and approach the pits from the south.

Access

Good roadside views over most of the western lake may be obtained
from the gateway which provides limited parking. When, in the late
afternoon or evening, light conditions are poor for viewing from this
angle, the public footpath (signposted to Warton) to the south of the
lake, just before the bridge over the Keer, offers a useful alternative.
It also allows views of the odd corners which are out of sight from
the road. Most of the near shore of the lake can be revealed by just
walking south along the road a short way. A telescope is required to
get the best from this site.

Habitat

Open fresh water, from flooding of disused gravel workings, and surrounding grazing land.

Birds

Any time of year:	great crested grebe, shoveler, sparrowhawk, kestrel, oystercatcher, lapwing, redshank, skylark, reed bunting.
Breeding season:	shelduck, common sandpiper, sedge warbler.
Winter visitors:	cormorant, grey heron, wigeon, gadwall, teal, pochard, tufted duck, scaup, long-tailed duck, goldeneye, smew, red-breasted merganser, goosander, snipe, common gull.
Passage migrants:	ringed plover, whimbrel, curlew, black tern, sand martin, meadow pipit, yellow wagtail.

This site is particularly notable for scarce wintering diving ducks. **Scaup, smew** and even **long-tailed duck** will sometimes overwinter and rarities include **ring-necked duck**. The same individual birds to be seen here often use the nearby water at the Pine Lake resort until disturbed by water sports. Some even commute as far as Leighton Moss, or use all three sites depending on weather conditions. Dockacres is on a migration route and is well known for birds passing through in spring. Waders, which may well include **whimbrel** on spring passage, frequent the shoreline and especially the few exposed rocks, sometimes forming a small island, over to the left (as viewed from the gateway). This can be viewed more closely from further down the road (a small gap in the hedge provides a convenient vantage point).

Marton Mere

Location

O.S. Landranger Series sheet 102 (Preston & Blackpool) grid reference SD334352.

Close to Blackpool Zoo and Stanley Park which are well signposted. From the road dividing the zoo from the park (the A587) turn down Lawson Road which is on the right before the zoo if travelling north.

Access

This is a nature reserve managed by Blackpool City Council. Free public access but all dogs to be kept on leads. It is possible to park near the end of Lawson Road and walk between the playing fields and the allotments to approach the reserve. Wellingtons are advisable at all times of year except after prolonged dry spells.

Habitat

Fresh water lake with an island and a small reedbed, scrub and rough grassland with a newly-created golf course. The lake is a natural feature although much reduced in size since drainage, which was begun before 1700.

Birds

Any time of year:	little grebe, great crested grebe, grey heron, pochard, tufted duck, ruddy duck, sparrowhawk, kestrel, grey partridge, lapwing, redshank, great black-backed gull, collared dove, little owl, skylark, greenfinch, goldfinch, linnet, reed bunting.
Breeding season:	common tern, grasshopper warbler, sedge warbler, reed warbler, whitethroat, willow warbler.
Winter visitors:	cormorant, Bewick's swan, shelduck, wigeon, teal, pintail, shoveler, scaup, goldeneye, water rail, jack snipe, snipe, woodcock, common gull, long-eared owl, short-eared owl, meadow pipit, stonechat, fieldfare.
Passage migrants:	garganey, common sandpiper, Mediterranean gull, sand martin, whinchat, wheatear.

At the far edge of the playing field, numerous muddy tracks lead through a marshy area to a good track: turn right to reach the reserve. (The wet part can be avoided by approaching from the main A587, but it is a long walk). Interesting birds can be seen in the scrubland before reaching the reserve itself, for example a wintering **stonechat** or **whitethroats** in summer. The wet fields on the right regularly hold **snipe**.

Carry straight on, past a small pumping station, to one of the entrances to the reserve. The rough grassland and scrub ahead to the left represent the owls' main hunting territory. It is not unusual to see a **short-eared owl** hunting in the thin light of a winter's

Sedge warblers sometimes nest in the same habitat as reed warblers but their bold supercilium and generally streaky appearance makes them easy to distinguish. (S. Craig.)

afternoon whereas **long-eared owls** are normally strictly nocturnal. They are unlikely to be seen in daylight except roosting in thick bushes and even then they can be notoriously hard to find, being so motionless and well camouflaged.

This SSSI (Site of Special Scientific Interest) has been damaged by the conversion of some of the rough grass fields to a golf course. There is now a more restricted area for owls to hunt over, but the precise impact on their success is difficult to determine as the number of owls present on the site varies dramatically from winter to winter. This is a natural phenomenon mainly dependent on their breeding success elsewhere, which in turn reflects the supply of their small rodent prey.

In summer the same area may be used by **grasshopper warblers** while **sedge** and **reed warblers** inhabit the reed bed on the right by the mere. It is best to continue right round the lake and view it from all angles. Some of the **ducks** tend to congregate on the shore of the island visible from the far side of the mere, near the caravan site. **Waders** may also be attracted to the shoreline of the island when the water level is relatively low. **Cormorants** often loaf on the wooden perches projecting from the water while **gulls** tend to roost in a flock on the lake itself.

Being so near the coast this site is well placed for migrants with the result that a good variety of scarce birds has been seen here. These include **ring-billed gull** (in winter), **white-winged black tern** (in summer), **spotted crake** (in autumn) and **Cetti's warbler** (which overwintered). There have also been some major rarities such as a **lesser yellowlegs**, on the same spring day as a **hoopoe**, and an **American bittern** (in winter). European **bitterns** from the continent are thought to winter here quite regularly, although I have not seen any. On no less than three occasions a bittern has been seen to rise from the marsh in spring, circle high until just a dot in the sky and then head off to the east.

6

The Lancashire Mosslands

In recent centuries extensive drainage has changed Lancashire's peat mosslands beyond all recognition. The current chapter refers to those areas still known as mosses and marked as such on modern maps although the vast majority of these places are farmland now and comprise the main regions of arable farming in Lancashire. Also included is Martin Mere which might seem to more logically belong in the freshwater wetland chapter; however it is perhaps more representative of the range of habitats traditionally associated with the mosses and it is principally important for wintering geese and swans which are the classic mossland specialities. The mosses have all been affected by drainage: even undrained ones will dry out by the general lowering of the water table unless active steps are taken as on a nature reserve. In our region the only sizeable area left in anything remotely like its original condition is Winmarleigh Moss. Being also a rare example of an uncultivated peat moss it deserves conservation basically for its plantlife. It is not however noted as being of special value for birds: in particular, flocks of geese roam over such a wide area that they are at least as likely to be found on other parts of the Fylde plain, possibly more so depending on crop availability (crops being generally more nutritious than natural vegetation) and bird-scaring devices. Martin Mere and the surrounding area is preferred because they are not disturbed and food is provided at the reserve. The vast majority of the geese which winter in Lancashire are pink-footed geese but a flock may sometimes contain a vagrant bean goose, whitefront or snow goose. What few brent geese there may be in the region tend to confine themselves to estuarine locations and are not generally attracted to the mosses.

The areas which later became the Lancashire mosslands, in common with most of the rest of Britain, were once covered with ancient forests. However, the sea encroached for several miles inland and swamped the low-lying coastal areas which eventually became fens and then peat bogs. There is evidence that some of these inundations were violent affairs with whole tracts of forest being swept away in one major incursion of the tide backed by a terrific storm. In addition to the raised bogs which subsequently formed over much of the coastal plain, there are occasional basin mires further inland but their associated birdlife is broadly similar. Raised bogs are usually only slightly convex in overall profile with small undulations over the region of active peat formation towards the centre. The drier portions typically sustain heather while wet grassland and carr are found near the edge of the bog which is often marked by a stream known as the lagg.

By the Middle Ages the landscape of the coastal plains was characterized by open fields with settlements on the higher ridges and large areas of mossland in between. At its driest extreme this included parts referred to as moors, which were used for rough summer grazing, while the wettest sections were the carrs (the word has a Norse origin meaning marsh overgrown by brushwood). These would have been the most ecologically productive regions comprising areas in various stages of natural succession between open water and scrub, alder and willow being typical. Hedges and mature trees were scarce, all significant woodland having been cleared by the start of the Anglo-Saxon period to make way for human habitation. Some drainage was already taking place in the Middle Ages and its main effect would have been to claim the edges of the moss for agriculture. Martin Mere, however, was untouched until towards the end of the seventeenth century and it is difficult for us to imagine from our current perspective, relying so much on road transport, how great a physical obstacle this vast impenetrable and extremely dangerous expanse of open water and marsh must have been.

The huge expanses of spongy wet peat moss itself, would have been a rather poor habitat for birds. Typical breeding species in such places are meadow pipit, skylark, reed bunting, mallard, curlew, cuckoo and snipe but they are all restricted to low densities. Twite used to be the exception as they were formerly abundant on mosslands but have declined dramatically. Our surviving lowland peat mosses are now worthy of protection more for their insects which include some rarities. On the other hand the marginal areas and the interspersed reed swamps with their richer, more varied fen vegetation would surely have supported a much wider variety of wetland and scrub species. As it is the whole mossland ecosystem has been extensively modified by human activities primarily for food production. Although the habitat is now mostly too dry for probing waders like curlew and snipe, there have been gains in other breeding species, more prevalent in drier farmland, such as whitethroat, linnet, corn bunting, yellowhammer and grey partridge. Red-legged partridge may also be present but are much scarcer and the situation is confused by the release of chukars and hybrids by gamekeepers. Any small wooded areas may provide nesting sites for kestrels and pigeons including stock doves and occasionally even turtle doves. In winter, besides the wild swans and geese already mentioned, fleeing the arctic north, several species feed on improved grassland, for example flocks of lapwing and golden plover, corvids, thrushes and starlings. Even the occasional great grey shrike may find a winter home on the mosses if there are a few scattered bushes to perch on.

The mosslands have long been home to barn owls which became commensurate with man ever since their rodent food supply increased as a result of grain availability from arable farming. Principally a tropical and mediterranean species, barn owls reach the northern limit of their range in Britain, with its maritime influence and consequently milder climate, and they naturally suffer a high mortality in severe winters. None the less barn owls were formerly common in Lancashire but have been much reduced in recent decades due to changing agricultural practices. Like other predatory birds, they have probably suffered from accumulated toxins derived from the former wholesale use of persistent pesticides. However their decline began long before other species were affected in this way, indicating that other causes may be primarily to blame for their demise. Their preferred nesting and roosting sites are disused buildings and hollow trees, especially old elm stumps, both of which have progressively been removed from the habitat during the period in question. Coupled with this, the rough grassland and hedgerows they used for hunting their main prey, the short-tailed vole, have also been displaced to make way for more intensive farming. Yet another reason for the decline of the barn owl may lie in the increased danger from modern fast-moving road traffic. Owls fly quite slowly, relying on silent flight and stealth rather than speed to catch their food, and collision with vehicles is now a major cause of death among barn owls. However they have recently fared better in Lancashire, due to sympathetic actions by farmers and others, and seem to be making something of a recovery. They are most likely to be seen hunting when food is in short supply in winter, especially when a covering of snow conceals their rodent prey, or when they have the demands of a hungry young brood to satisfy.

Little owls are characteristic of predominantly rural habitats at various altitudes, mosslands included, and again are often associated with quiet undisturbed buildings. They are much more likely to be seen by day than barn owls and like to warm themselves in the morning sun. They often disappear for the middle of the day but re-emerge during the late afternoon. Once a little owl has been seen in

*Formerly common on Lancashire mosslands, barn owls have declined
rapidly due mainly to altered farming methods. However action is being
taken and the future now looks somewhat brighter for this ethereal species.
(S. Craig.)*

a particular place it is well worth looking again in the same spot as individuals can be very faithful to chosen sites. The commonest avian predator of open habitats such as the mosses is the familiar kestrel which frequently hovers in search of small rodents. In this attitude, with its tail lowered for balance, the black sub-terminal band is often clearly visible on the underside of the tail. On the adult male bird this contrasts well with the plain grey tail and confirms its identity even from a distance.

Songbirds are also in evidence on the mosslands, including whitethroats which can be regarded as the archetypal warblers of low open scrubland. Hedgerows may provide a substitute scrub habitat from where the song may be delivered: it has a similar structural form to the dunnock's song but with a diagnostic scratchy tone. Corn buntings have declined over much of Britain but are still relatively common on the Lancashire mosslands. In the breeding season they will habitually sing from a high exposed perch, telephone wires being a favourite, enabling easy observation. They can clearly be seen to throw back the head to give their short but characteristic jangling song which starts with a few discrete ticks before the trill gets underway. In winter they form flocks, still perching on the wires from where they fly down to feed in the fields when it appears safe.

Martin Mere

Location

O.S. Landranger Series sheet 108 (Liverpool) grid reference SD429144.

A nature reserve belonging to the Wildfowl and Wetlands Trust. Signposted on the brown signs for tourist attractions although shorter routes are ignored if not suitable for coaches. From Rufford, on the A59, take the B5246 west, signposted to Martin Mere. Turn left shortly (but not sharp left which leads back to the A59) on either of the next two roads which join after about 700m. Once onto the open moss fork left onto Curlew Lane. Turn right at the end (about 1.5km) and the reserve entrance is on the left after a further 1km.

Access

Large car park on gravel area with extension to adjoining grass at peak times. Can get very busy in summer on Sundays and at bank holiday weekends. There is an occasional bus service from Ormskirk (Monday to Saturday) and from Southport (Wednesdays only in summer). Non-members of the Wildfowl and Wetlands Trust are charged for entrance to the reserve. The nearer bird hides are accessible by wheelchair.

Facilities

Toilets including facilities for the disabled; café; gift shop.

Habitat

As well as being an SSSI, this is a Ramsar site and a Special Protection Area. Open fresh water with islands, including many shallow parts and some areas of shingle; dykes, banks and marshes; hedgerows and a few bushes; the mossland around is farmed as rough grazing and arable land. Formerly the largest lake in Lancashire (some 5km across), the mere of today is but a tiny re-created image of a vast natural expanse of open water and marsh. Drainage, attempted from 1692 onwards but largely ineffective until 1781, was completed by 1849.

Birds

Any time of year:	grey heron, shelduck, wigeon, gadwall, teal, shoveler, pochard, tufted duck, kestrel, grey partridge, lapwing, ruff, snipe, stock dove, collared dove, barn owl, kingfisher, skylark, long-tailed tit, goldfinch, reed bunting, corn bunting.
Breeding season:	marsh harrier, oystercatcher, little ringed plover, black-tailed godwit, redshank, common tern, cuckoo, sedge warbler, lesser whitethroat, willow warbler.
Winter visitors:	cormorant, Bewick's swan, whooper swan, bean goose, pink-footed goose, white-fronted goose, barnacle goose, American wigeon, pintail, scaup, hen harrier, sparrowhawk, merlin, peregrine, golden plover, short-eared owl, fieldfare, redwing, greenfinch, siskin.
Passage migrants:	garganey, ringed plover, little stint, curlew sandpiper, dunlin, curlew, greenshank, green sandpiper, wood sandpiper, common sandpiper, sand martin, blackcap.

In the reception building the first thing for the keen birdwatcher to take note of are the lists of wild birds seen recently on the reserve (and sometimes nearby if there is something special around). There are further lists outside some of the hides, the New Raines Observatory and Millers Bridge Hide in particular. One of the advantages of a reserve like this is that it is well watched by the wardens and many experienced birders, so that a rarity will seldom go unnoticed for long: you are encouraged to add relevant information of your own to the lists of recent sightings. Vast numbers of birds are attracted to the sanctuary by the first-class habitat and the food provided so, besides being quite a spectacle in its own right, it is hardly surprising that rarities will turn up amongst them from time to time. For example the huge flock of **wigeon**, which often reaches over twenty thousand in mid winter, has been found to contain an **American wigeon** on several occasions over the years.

The door to the grounds leads initially to the wildfowl collection of species from all over the world, which obviously has a lot of interest although outside the scope of this book on wild birds. Of course wild birds do use the collection area, especially where food is distributed, and any birds other than wildfowl (ducks, geese and swans) and fla-mingos are likely to have flown there by their own volition. In theory everything beyond the collection area is wild, but in practice the situation is confused by the presence of free-flying feral birds of some species, notably barnacle and greylag geese, mandarin duck, gold-eneye and even gadwall. Most of these species originate from the collection but feral greylag and Canada geese are always quick to take advantage of an easy artificial source of food and could have come from anywhere. Mandarin duck exist in the 'wild' in Britain only as feral birds anyway but with species which have natural British populations, or are known to be occasional visitors, birders are keen to determine their origin. If in doubt as to the status of particular birds discuss the matter with one of the wardens, whom I have found very helpful. One time a **cackling Canada goose** was present which was clearly of a different race from the rest of the Canada geese and was taken to be a genuine transatlantic vagrant.

As can be seen from the map on the notice board in the Centre, the hides are set around three sides of the nature reserve. To reach them, turn to the right from the collection and proceed through a gate in the high fence to meet the connecting path. The best hides for seeing the hundreds of wild swans, including the Swan Link Hide, are along this straight section. This is the only guaranteed site in Lancashire for wintering **Bewick's** and **whooper swans**, and very

A rare winter visitor to Lancashire, the occasional lesser whitefront might be found amongst the large flocks of pinkfeet. (S. Craig.)

close views are ensured by the feeding régime. This strategy tends to attract the wildfowl away from neighbouring farmland, thus reducing crop damage and tensions with local farmers.

Wild **geese** are attracted in their thousands but, as they often feed in the surrounding fields, the best hide to view them from may be the Greater Manchester Hide or Millers Bridge Hide depending on their position and that of the sun, if any. These two hides are at the extreme ends of the path but are physically closer together than it might appear. Surplus root crops are sometimes dumped near the Hale Hide (to the right when facing the reserve, on the way to Millers Bridge) and these may be a major attraction for the geese. They consist almost entirely of **pink-footed geese** but odd stragglers of other species occasionally get mixed up in the flock. Both **bean geese** and **whitefronts** have major wintering areas in southern England which may explain why these two species seem to be more regular at Martin Mere on spring passage (often in late April or even into May) than as winter visitors.

Martin Mere is probably the most likely place in Lancashire to see a **barn owl**, sometimes even hunting by day: from 2:30 onwards on a still afternoon in winter affords a fair chance. Millers Bridge Hide offers the best vantage point for many of the specialities including **owls** and **birds of prey**, although the Greater Manchester Hide has given some exceptionally close views of **barn owl**, **merlin** and **sparrowhawk** at times. Stretched out in front of Millers Bridge Hide are Sunleys and Vinsons marshes which hold most of the **ducks** and **waders**. The trouble is that many of the birds spend much of their time away in the distance and, especially with waders, it is often tricky to identify the smaller ones even with a powerful telescope. **Kingfishers** are more obliging, sometimes perching over the dyke just in front of the hide, on a water pipe or on the bridge itself.

Sometimes an unusual wader may be seen closer from another hide: the shallow edges of the mere itself, with its many islands, can keep a small wader busy for hours, while the small pool in front of the Hale Hide occasionally attracts **green** and **wood sandpipers** in particular. On the same side of the mere, slightly nearer the Centre, is the New Raines Observatory which is a modern hide with chairs, and heated in winter, from which birdwatching in comfort is possible. The hedge and bushes along this side of the reserve tend to get most of the songbirds such as **redwing**, **long-tailed tit** and **siskin** in winter, or **warblers** on passage.

Most of the scarce birds I have seen at Martin Mere seem to have been in the summer and autumn. **Red-necked phalarope** and **Temminck's stint** have occurred in both May, and July which is often thought of as the quietest month for birdwatching; **spoonbill** and **spotted crake** in August; **blue-winged teal** and **Wilson's phalarope** in September; and **lesser white-fronted goose** in October. To anyone living locally who would like a chance to see such exciting birds, I would recommend joining the Wildfowl and Wetlands Trust to take advantage of the free entrance for members to their Centres such as Martin Mere.

The South-Western Mosslands

Location

O.S. Landranger Series sheet 108 (Liverpool) grid references: see below.

A somewhat nebulous zone of mosses towards the southern extremity of Lancashire.

Access

A relevant O.S. map is essential in order to come to terms with this area. The main access routes are the minor roads which cross the mosses and a few public footpaths. Parking on these narrow lanes without obstructing agricultural traffic is awkward. For example, there are just one or two places by the roadside along Plex Moss Lane, which is about central to the main region and runs from the A5147 at SD363091 to Woodvale on the A565.

Habitat

Low-lying flat farmland with some remnant peat moss; brooks and drainage dykes; a few scattered copses and small woods.

Birds

Any time of year: kestrel, grey partridge, lapwing, stock dove, collared dove, barn owl, great spotted wood-pecker, skylark, tree sparrow, greenfinch, gold-finch, linnet, yellowhammer, corn bunting.

Breeding season: shelduck, oystercatcher, cuckoo, yellow wag-tail, whitethroat.

Winter visitors: grey heron, Bewick's swan, whooper swan, pink-footed goose, white-fronted goose, snow goose, hen harrier, golden plover, common gull, meadow pipit, fieldfare.

Passage migrants: wheatear.

The principal region under this heading is bounded by Southport and the A565 on the west; the River Alt to the south; the A5147, from Lydiate through Haskayne and Halsall to Scarisbrick, on the east; and the B5243 to the north. This includes Halsall Moss, Plex Moss, Downholland Moss and The Withins, and is a large area to cover adequately but the typical birds to be found are similar through-out. Also included in the above list are birds seen in the region sur-rounding Martin Mere and an outlying, perhaps less typical, area near Roby's Farm, Bickerstaffe (grid reference SD435036). In winter some of the **Bewick's** and **whooper swans** from Martin Mere leave the reserve at times and may be seen feeding locally, especially on the fields to either side of Curlew Lane (see directions to Martin Mere).

One of the main mossland specialities is the winter flocks of

In spite of extensive drainage the south-west Lancashire mosslands still attract large numbers of birds especially in winter.

pink-footed geese, always with the possibility of a rare straggler, for instance a **whitefront**, amongst them. However, because most of the geese are in large flocks, they are to be seen in only a limited number of places at any given time. A useful technique is to survey the mosses from a suitable elevated position such as a bridge over the disused railway line: those on New Cut Lane (at SD361116) and on the lane between Haskayne and Formby (at SD344080) may be found most helpful. A casual visit at any time of year is likely to yield the common mossland species, namely **corn bunting**, **kestrel** and **grey partridge**. The last may often be heard at dusk giving their far-carrying creaky call which sounds rather eerie in the twilight. **Stock doves** are relatively common in these parts and sometimes even perch on wires with woodpigeons for handy comparison. In spring and summer the scene is enlivened by the enthusiastic song of the **whitethroat** while migration may bring in **wheatears**. Under favourable conditions there might be quite a few in the same field, each one conspicuous in turn as it suddenly hops along a few paces and then stands bolt upright again.

Croston and Mawdesley Mosses

Location

O.S. Landranger Series sheet 108 (Liverpool) grid reference SD487149.

Lying immediately to the east of Rufford, on a line between Chorley and Southport, this is a roughly circular area, about 4km across, without any through roads. There are several possible approaches but the reference given above is of the Mawdesley end of a public footpath running north—south across the middle of these mosses. From Rufford on the A59, take the B5246 east towards Parbold. After crossing the Leeds and Liverpool Canal, the railway line and the River Douglas, turn left along Blackmoor Road (the first main road, about 1.5km from Rufford). After another 1.5km there is a public footpath sign on the left (near another 'Blackmoor Road' sign).

Access

The roadside verge is just wide enough to take a small car. Alternatively, the footpath can be reached from the north end, there being more room to park in the back streets of Croston near the River Yarrow. The western edge of the moss can be covered from the canal towpath between the B5246 and the A581 to Chorley, and this is the area where a **great grey shrike** chose to spend most of one winter recently.

Habitat

Although this area has been extensively drained to support more intensive agriculture, it still presents quite a varied tapestry of different crops and fallow fields, a few copses, some hedgerows with scattered trees, and odd uncultivated corners.

Birds

Any time of year:	kestrel, grey partridge, lapwing, stock dove, collared dove, barn owl, little owl, great spotted woodpecker, skylark, long-tailed tit, jay, greenfinch, linnet, yellowhammer, reed bunting, corn bunting.
Breeding season:	shelduck, quail, oystercatcher, turtle dove, cuckoo, whitethroat.
Winter visitors:	fieldfare, great grey shrike.

Flocks of fieldfares, with variable numbers of redwings, roam the mosslands in winter feeding mainly on soil invertebrates. (B. Marsh.)

Walk down the track between the houses and the second time it takes a right angle bend to the left, follow the public footpath straight on. At this point, scan along the roofs of the dilapidated barns to the left for a **little owl**, especially at dusk but also sometimes in broad daylight. Continue to a series of thick wooden posts along the path: this is the middle of Croston and Mawdesley mosses. I generally return at this point but the public right of way goes through to Croston and there are numerous other footpaths over the mosslands here, although harder to find.

Quail are unusual summer migrants in that their breeding range varies dramatically from year to year depending on the weather conditions. If there is a lot of hot dry weather in late spring they may reach as far north as southern Scotland whereas in a poor year they may fall short of Lancashire altogether. However in a good year, this site is as likely a place as any to hear them calling at dusk and dawn, and sometimes on into the morning, from the tall crops they inhabit. This territorial call is an incessantly repeated triple note with the first of the group separated and the others very close together, producing a most characteristic rhythm. The sounds have a distinctive ringing quality reminiscent in tone of those from a nuthatch. Although they may sound so close, the birds themselves are almost never seen except occasionally on migration if accidentally flushed from some more general habitat.

This is a good area for **buntings**, where all the usual species can be seen in close proximity, and offers a useful opportunity to learn their different songs in spring and early summer.

The Fylde Mosslands

Location

O.S. Landranger Series sheet 102 (Preston & Blackpool) grid references: see below.

By using the above map there is plenty of scope for finding your own favourite spots but I have enjoyed some good birdwatching towards the eastern edge of Winmarleigh Moss (for example near SD464490); near Bond's Farm (SD483424); and on Pilling Moss, especially near Scronkey (at SD410470). The region around Nateby (2km west of Garstang) can also produce some worthwhile species.

Access

As in the south-western mosslands, finding somewhere sensible to park can be a problem in some places. Access on roads and public footpaths: the Pilling area is more liberally endowed with footpaths than some of the larger mosses, enabling more thorough coverage.

Habitat

Predominantly flat arable and dairy farming land with just a tiny fraction of the original peat remaining; significant areas can still flood under torrential winter rains; some parts with isolated copses; hedgerows rather more prevalent than in the south-western mosslands.

Birds

Any time of year:	sparrowhawk, kestrel, grey partridge, lapwing, curlew, stock dove, collared dove, barn owl, little owl, skylark, tree sparrow, yellowhammer, reed bunting, corn bunting.
Breeding season:	oystercatcher, whitethroat.
Winter visitors:	cormorant, grey heron, Bewick's swan, whooper swan, pink-footed goose, snow goose, barnacle goose, golden plover, common gull, meadow pipit, fieldfare, redwing.

Although there are other mossland areas (which may provide fruitful birdwatching) on the Fylde plain, the region covered here is that known as Over Wyre, being virtually enclosed by the River Wyre as it wends its tortuous course to the sea. The boundary to the west can be regarded as being the B5272 from Garstang to Cockerham and the A588 as far as Conder Green since a huge flock of **pink-footed geese** sometimes uses the area around Norbreck Farm (grid reference SD452535) in winter. The geese range widely over the mosses in flocks both large and small and locating them on a particular day is a skill in itself. They favour areas well away from disturbance wherever the feeding is good, and may frequent a particular field until the food source is exhausted (perhaps several days) before moving on elsewhere. Much of the terrain away from the coastal strip is gently undulating and Eagland Hill, such as it is, provides a fairly central vantage point (grid reference SD430453). Another technique depends on trying to judge where an airborne flock will land: pinkfeet have a characteristic call, with a high-pitched second syllable, which carries well and often draws attention to a flock in flight. A further possibility to consider is that of using a bicycle instead of a car. This certainly solves the parking problem but the price is sacrificed concealment since geese are quite easily disturbed and a car can be effectively used as a hide. However the slightly increased elevation on a cycle is a significant advantage when looking over hedges for a flock of birds at ground level, besides being far safer than scanning the fields whilst driving!

Wild **swans** may be found in similar situations to geese but are especially attracted to any floods. In winter most of the birds will be in flocks, other examples being **golden plover**, often mixed with **lapwing**, and buntings and finches which may include **tree sparrows**.

7

Uplands

Broadly speaking the further north and west ones goes in Britain, the more rugged and mountainous is the terrain encountered. Here in Lancashire we have no real mountains to compare with those of Scotland, the highest point in the heartland of the county being only 561m above sea level, near Ward's Stone in the Forest of Bowland. (The highest land currently in Lancashire is in fact at 627m on Leck Fell, near the extreme north-eastern tip of the county, but geographically it seems rather anomalous that this is not part of North Yorkshire.) Nevertheless about 13.5 per cent of the total area of Lancashire is classified as moorland. The boundary between the enclosed grassland of the highest farms and the open moorland is often ill defined, with much marginal land, but typically occurs from 300m to 350m in altitude. In exposed areas on the western edges of the uplands this transition zone can be lowered significantly to between 150m and 200m, while in other regions it may lie at over 400m. The situation is further complicated by reversion towards moorland of previously enclosed land which has since been abandoned. If this makes the definition of uplands somewhat subjective, any division based purely on altitude must be equally arbitrary. However the 300m level is frequently adopted as a convenient dividing line which corresponds nicely to where breeding blackbirds are traditionally supposed to give way to ring ouzels, although the latter can be found lower down in places.

The largest continuous region of upland habitat in Lancashire is the Forest of Bowland (SSSI) which is internationally important for breeding birds and the only regular breeding area in England for hen harrier. Where the ground is permanently sodden through high rainfall, peat can develop resulting in blanket bog which is the preferred habitat for golden plover and dunlin. The geology of uplands tends towards acidic rocks which, together with the leaching of nutrients, creates very infertile soils. The natural vegetation in these areas, excluding the waterlogged parts, consists of trees which are progressively dwarfed as exposure increases at higher altitudes, degenerating eventually into woody scrub. The true montane zone is never reached in Lancashire but begins at the natural limit of the scrub cover. However, this pattern of vegetation has been dramatically altered by human activities involving felling the trees followed by grazing and periodic burning, which prevents natural regeneration of the forest. These changes took place many centuries ago and have resulted in the moorland landscape we still know today. Most of the birds which we now regard as characteristic moorland species actually prefer to nest in relatively short vegetation and thus benefit from a régime of moderate grazing and controlled burning. On the other hand excessively frequent burning damages heather, an important plant for many moorland birds including ring ouzel and twite, and encourages other plants to dominate. Overgrazing also suppresses heather as can be observed in the West Pennine Moors, yet these changes are reversible with appropriate management.

Much of the moorland in Lancashire is maintained for rearing red grouse which feed principally on the fresh growth of heather. Hence this practice necessitates the keeping of healthy heather moors and is generally beneficial to other moorland species, although illegal persecution of birds which may prey on the grouse is still a problem in some areas. Not surprisingly the breeding density of red grouse is strongly influenced by the proportion of the moor covered by heather. However, where base-rich underlying rocks are present, more fertile conditions prevail and such moors, known as rich moors, hold up to twice the density of red grouse for the same degree of heather cover. Golden plover breeding densities also depend on the fertility of the soil with the maximum recorded being on limestone grassland areas in the Pennines. Physical features of the habitat are important to other species such as the availability of crags for nesting peregrines. Ring ouzels prefer areas which contain some crags, scree or boulders while wheatears favour short grass for feeding. By contrast, 'soft' moorland is an optimal habitat for ground-nesting merlin, hen harrier, short-eared owl, curlew, dunlin and golden plover. Because the uplands are so variable, the most widespread species are those with the least specialized requirements and the prime example must be the ubiquitous meadow pipit. Skylarks are almost as common but they show a preference for nesting in grass.

Very few birds can survive the rigours of winter on the fells. Red grouse is the most sedentary species: only in the most severe weather will they move appreciably from their home range. In winter they generally outnumber any other species in this habitat. Meadow pipits and skylarks are still there but in much reduced abundance, other species typically visible being wren, carrion crow and kestrel. A scarce winter visitor to Lancashire sometimes seen in upland areas as well as at coastal locations is the snow bunting, usually encountered in

small flocks. Birds of prey tend to resort to the coast in winter but
not necessarily for the whole time: some will commute depending on
the prevailing weather conditions and occasional sightings of the
rarer species are still made in upland regions, merlins and peregrines
seeming to favour clear frosty days.

The relatively inaccessible situation of uplands affords this kind
of habitat with more protection than most others. In addition over
forty per cent of Lancashire's moorland area is covered by SSSIs,
mainly the Forest of Bowland. Reclamation of land on the edges
of upland regions for farming has occurred from time to time but
does not pose a threat to significant areas of moorland in Lancashire. It is frequently temporary in nature and in any case the
marginal land itself is often important for birds such as tree pipit,
whinchat, waders or a hunting merlin. Paradoxically perhaps, one
of the greatest potential threats to moorland habitat in recent times
is afforestation. This process is nothing akin to the replacement of
the natural forests since commercial forestry has traditionally involved a dense block of trees, of an alien coniferous species, all at
the same age. In the early stages of growth some moorland birds,
and other species, can adapt and even thrive in the scrub-like conditions but, once the canopy closes in and excludes light to the
ground, these temporary colonists vanish as the mature forest
takes over. While such forests do harbour significant populations
of certain species, notably goldcrest and coal tit, their value to
wildlife is limited, chiefly by lack of diversity. Where a plantation
extends over a vast area of former moorland, the term blanket afforestation is applied and the population levels of characteristic upland bird species will drop to virtually zero.

On the other hand, it is possible to integrate commercial forestry
in the uplands with nature conservation. The densities of birds on
British moorlands are highly variable so the first requirement is to
avoid selecting for afforestation an area which is particularly valuable
in its current state. Among the upland species which have taken
advantage of certain aspects of conifer forestry as an alternative or
extension to their more natural habitat, are hen harrier, short-eared
owl and tree pipit. The success of these birds within regions of working
forest depends on sympathetic management. The harriers and owls
hunt over recently felled areas, while tree pipits favour places which
are still basically open, but with scattered trees to act as song posts.
Hence the key to maximizing the value of commercial forestry to
wildlife in general, and birds in particular, is the maintenance of a
diverse age structure among the trees in a given plot. There also

needs to be a clear access route to these various areas from the open moorland: an isolated pocket of suitable habitat buried deep inside a large mature forest is unlikely to be of much advantage to birds. The coniferous areas which are managed more constructively for wildlife have generally been made accessible to the public as nature trails and include part of Gisburn Forest (the largest tract of forest in our region) while other areas, of pure commercial forestry, tend to be inaccessible to the public or at least not well publicized.

Although I have yet to see any, goshawks also breed in the uplands of Lancashire, closely associated with coniferous plantations, but it is unwise to disclose any precise localities as they are still illegally persecuted by egg collectors, a few irresponsible falconers and maybe some misguided gamekeepers. These birds are mainly the descendants of individuals escaped from falconry, game keeping interests having exterminated the wild goshawk population in this country by the beginning of the twentieth century. There are several well-known favourite sites for birders to look for them although the actual nesting areas do sometimes vary from year to year.

One further type of habitat present in upland regions is provided by reservoirs. There are 118 of these currently within Lancashire, with a total surface area of over 1000ha, mostly concentrated in the south-east of the county. Many of the east Lancashire reservoirs have an upland character even though only a few are actually situated above the 300m contour. They all contain fish, some being regularly stocked by the angling clubs which use them. Although not generally known for being of special bird interest, they do attract their share of various species which dive for their food. Of particular interest are occasional records of apparently healthy divers which are not restricted to times of difficult weather at sea.

Wycoller and the Brontë Way

Location

O.S. Landranger Series sheet 103 (Blackburn & Burnley) grid reference SD926395.

This area lies at the heart of The Forest of Trawden, near the eastern extremity of Lancashire. From Trawden follow the brown tourists' signposts to Wycoller Country Park.

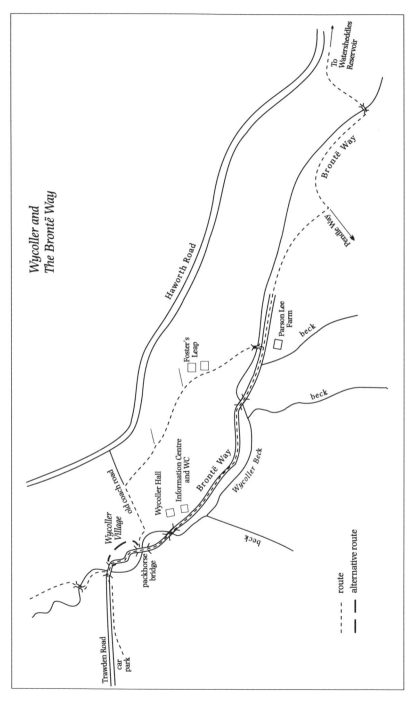

Wycoller and The Brontë Way

Access

At the end of the road is a large car park: vehicular access to the village of Wycoller is for residents only. Up on the main road, which runs into West Yorkshire, there is an alternative car park at Height Laithe to where a Leisure Links bus service runs from Rawtenstall, Burnley, Brierfield, Nelson, Colne and Laneshaw Bridge.

Facilities

Toilets (including provision for the disabled), café, information centre.

Habitat

Stream with bushes and trees along the valley; rough grazing land with transition to open moorland. Much of this site is a borderline upland region.

Birds

Any time of year:	sparrowhawk, kestrel, red grouse, lapwing, stock dove, collared dove, tawny owl, great spotted woodpecker, meadow pipit, dipper, coal tit, treecreeper, greenfinch, goldfinch, reed bunting.
Breeding season:	curlew, redshank, cuckoo, grey wagtail, redstart, wheatear, willow warbler, spotted flycatcher.
Winter visitors:	grey heron, fieldfare, redwing, goldcrest, siskin, redpoll.
Passage migrants:	whinchat, pied flycatcher.

There are many public paths around this area, as indicated on the various maps displayed outside the Aisled Barn Information Centre in Wycoller village. Note that the Brontë Way and the Pendle Way partially overlap which is a possible source of confusion. All these paths are suitable for birdwatching but the route I recommend leads through a variety of habitats and so provides a good cross-section of the local bird community.

Start by following the footpath alongside the road into the village, joining the road for the descent to the first bridge. I have found **dippers** and **wagtails** surprisingly difficult to locate here but they are around so it is always worth looking up and down the stream whenever it is in view. From here one can turn left to follow Wycoller Beck down part of the Pendle Way. Woodland edges the stream for a while and a variety of arboreal birds may be seen such as **great spotted woodpecker** and **treecreeper**.

Back at the first bridge continue along the road, or alternatively the footpath up behind it, to the pack-horse bridge. Close by are the ruins of Wycoller Hall and a good variety of **songbirds** can often be found feeding amongst the trees and bushes just above. A path leads up some stone steps opposite the pack-horse bridge and joins the old coach road running up to Height Laithe. Of historic interest all around this region are the upright slabs of stone which are the remnants of walls for retaining stock on medieval cattle farms called vaccaries. After the steepest part of the climb a footpath crosses the old coach road. Turn right here (labelled 'walk 3') over a stile to track across the side of the valley which is a region of rough grassland. Look out for **wheatears** and **redstarts** on the dry stone walls. In spring the calls of **cuckoos** may also be heard echoing down the valley. Keep on level at a fork rather than uphill to the left. Around here abundant thistle seeds attract twittering charms of **goldfinches** to feed in late summer. Continue past Foster's Leap Farm and after the next stile the path becomes indistinct but head down slightly to the right to cross the beck on a wooden footbridge and join the main track near Parson Lee Farm.

Following the marked route from the farm takes one up Smithy Clough and out to the open moors. About 650m past the farm the path meets a track (Brontë/Pendle Way). Turn left here to follow the Brontë Way which ascends onto a plateau of heather moorland. Elsewhere **red grouse** may be more often heard than seen but here they are so plentiful that flocks will sometimes take to the air at once showing the silvery underside to their whirring wings. Return by the same route to Parson Lee Farm and simply follow the main track back downstream to Wycoller.

Gisburn Forest and Stocks Reservoir

Location

O.S. Landranger Series sheet 103 (Blackburn & Burnley) grid reference SD732565.

Isolated position in north-eastern Lancashire, to the east of the Forest of Bowland proper. From Slaidburn take the B6478 towards Long Preston for about 5km before turning left at a crossroads (by a telephone kiosk). Follow this road for another 3km and the entrance to the car park is on a sharp right-hand bend.

Access

Ample free parking and public access on paths within the forest area, including waymarked routes.

Habitat

An extensive coniferous plantation with a reasonably varied age structure, a few deciduous trees in places, and scattered farmsteads. Close by is a large reservoir with an island.

Birds

Any time of year: hen harrier, sparrowhawk, kestrel, red grouse, lapwing, woodcock, stock dove, short-eared owl, great spotted woodpecker, goldcrest, long-tailed tit, coal tit, treecreeper, goldfinch, redpoll, crossbill, bullfinch.

Breeding season: red-breasted merganser, curlew, common sandpiper, cuckoo, tree pipit.

Winter visitors: cormorant, grey heron, wigeon, teal, pochard, tufted duck, goldeneye, goosander, fieldfare, siskin.

The bird species are fairly clearly divided between the water birds on and around the reservoir, some of which may be viewed only distantly, and the birds of the forested region for which this site is most interesting. **Short-eared owls, kestrels** and **hen harriers** may been seen hunting the recently felled areas, not exclusively in the breeding season but also during milder weather in winter. In summer, **tree pipits** can be found in places where scattered trees are becoming established again after felling. The exact location of these differing parts will obviously change over time but, with numerous public footpaths and tracks through the forest, one need not be limited to the circular routes, colour marked on posts, although these could be a good starting point. I would certainly recommend going as far as the outlying farms: the area between Hindley Head and Tenters (see O.S. map) has proved most fruitful. To see **red grouse** it would be necessary to continue right up onto the open moors.

Bottoms Beck, one of the feeder streams for the reservoir, descends through the forest and in places along the valley there is a greater variety of tree species. These are among the spots most frequented by the small arboreal birds, such as **redpolls**. The beck joins an extended arm of the reservoir which is crossed by the approach road

Short-eared owls may be seen during the day quartering the more open areas within and around Gisburn Forest, hunting for their main prey, short-tailed field voles. (S. Craig.)

on a causeway. This is a good place to look for **common sandpipers** in summer.

The island in the reservoir is significant because of the protection it affords to breeding birds from ground predators, hence the large breeding colony of **black-headed gulls**.

Langden Valley

Location

O.S. Landranger Series sheet 102 (Preston & Blackpool) grid reference SD632512.

Within the Forest of Bowland SSSI (Site of Special Scientific Interest). The starting point is on the road through the Trough of Bowland, 3km from Dunsop Bridge.

Access

Ample free parking by the roadside at the start of the trail. This area gets busy on fine Sunday afternoons and bank holidays, even to the extent of traffic jams on the single-track road! The walk is quiet, however, as few people venture far from their cars.

Facilities

The nearest public toilets are in Dunsop Bridge.

Habitat

Upland river valley, moorland, developing scrub/wooded patches, small planted area.

Birds

Any time of year: buzzard, kestrel, red grouse, meadow pipit, goldcrest, coal tit, treecreeper.

Breeding season: hen harrier, peregrine, oystercatcher, curlew, common sandpiper, cuckoo, short-eared owl, tree pipit, grey wagtail, redstart, whinchat, wheatear, ring ouzel, willow warbler, spotted flycatcher.

The route begins on a tarmac track through an avenue of sycamores and rhododendrons to the North West Water Langden intake. Near the end of the small strip of larches to the left is a favourite haunt of **spotted flycatchers** in summer. Around the intake area is also a likely place to see **grey wagtails** on Langden Brook.

Once past 'civilization' and out into the open, any of the characteristic upland species are possible during the summer months. Pipits are common here and by far the easiest way to distinguish the two species is by the much more varied and far-carrying song of the **tree pipit**, which is often delivered from the top of a small tree as well as in the typical

A view of the path up Langden Valley in the Forest of Bowland, an excellent area for seeing a good variety of upland species.

song flight. Tree pipits require such scattered bushes in their habitat while **meadow pipits** use open moorland with only ground vegetation.

About 2km past the intake the track turns sharply right then left (while a small private track doubles back to the right). A relatively level patch on the right at this point forms a sort of tiny plateau on which a **ring ouzel** might be seen feeding, while **redstarts** have been observed in the stunted trees growing up the slope beyond, towards the ridge. **Ring ouzels** usually begin their arrival in Britain from the end of March and can often be located whilst in song until about mid June. They tend to sing from exposed perches such as the corner of a rocky outcrop or high in a tree but are otherwise quite secretive birds. All that can normally be heard of the song from a distance is a doleful piping note usually given three times.

It is from this stage onwards that the various **birds of prey** are more likely to be seen although **kestrels** frequently hover over the ridges all along the route. Hunting **hen harriers** seem to float round the valleys as if following invisible contour lines. Unfortunately they are not as common as they should be due to persecution by the gamekeeping interest. This area is intensively managed for **red grouse** and many harrier nests have been destroyed over the years in spite of full legal protection.

Where the public footpath diverges from the track, follow the marker posts and use the boardwalks to escape the wettest parts. The path leads down to the brook where the energetic may like to follow it across on stepping stones and up the valley opposite. Although the right of way continues right through to Bleasdale it is nearly always so saturated on the top that wellingtons are essential. However, it is straightforward to follow it far enough to obtain a good view over Webster's Meadow to the left, on the far side of the valley, where **hen harriers** may often be seen hunting or soaring on thermals.

Pendle Hill

Location

O.S. Landranger Series sheet 103 (Blackburn & Burnley) grid reference SD814417.

This site lies within a discrete section of the Forest of Bowland CMA (Countryside Management Area) which is also designated as an AONB (Area of Outstanding Natural Beauty). From the A59 trunk road heading towards Skipton, take a minor road on the right to Worston, 4.3km after the Clitheroe roundabout. Continue for 3.5km through Worston to the outskirts of Downham and there turn sharp right to head uphill. After another 3.5km turn right again at the crossroads on the open moors. Just over 1km further on, park by the start of the track to Pendle Side Farm.

Access

Parking space for several cars on the gravel by the roadside. Access on public paths as indicated by the signs.

Facilities

Public toilets at Barley, 1.7km further down the hill.

Habitat

Upland farm and moorland.

Birds

Any time of year: sparrowhawk, kestrel, merlin, red grouse, little owl, meadow pipit.

*Variable numbers of dotterel return each spring to Pendle Hill briefly
gracing the moors with their subtle beauty before continuing to their arctic
breeding grounds. (B. Marsh.)*

Breeding season: golden plover, lapwing, curlew, redshank,
                        cuckoo, skylark, wheatear, ring ouzel, gold-
                        finch, linnet, twite.

Winter visitors: snow bunting.

Passage migrants: dotterel, black redstart, stonechat.

The footpath up the hill is well signposted from the track to the farm.
Pendle Hill is the most well-known haunt of **dotterel** on spring migration in Lancashire. These attractive birds are renowned for being
faithful to particular migration sites although in cold wet springs they
are perhaps more likely to be found on the lowland mosses than at
this altitude. Dependent to some extent on the weather, the first week
in May is often the best time for maximum numbers which in a good
year can peak at around a score or more. By mid May any left tend
to be flighty. The area most often favoured is the sloping stony plateau
to the south-west of the summit which can most easily be approached
from the left-hand path where it divides by a sign with the Pendle
Witches motif, near the base of the hill. On the way up, a likely place

to see migrating **ring ouzels** is along the stone wall to the left. Where the path reaches the top, it curves right round and cairns mark the way to the triangulation point. About a right angle around this curve, the bottom of the stony plateau frequented by the **dotterel** lies straight ahead. They are quite tame if approached cautiously and usually give a patient observer some really close views. They are also surprisingly well camouflaged and can be difficult to pick out among the stones especially when there are only a few birds present which may be temporarily hidden in the small dips. It thus pays to scan the area carefully since, if flushed, they may depart to another part of the hill for several hours. By the same token, it is best to be up the hill early in the morning before they may have been disturbed by anyone else.

Other species to be seen from near the summit include **red grouse** which breed quite commonly here and **golden plover** which may first be revealed by their plaintive whistles. Quick reactions are required to see **merlins** which fly fast and low and so are not often in view for long in this type of terrain. The **twite** are generally found on the lower slopes, perhaps feeding among the bracken (when this dies back in winter it assumes the appearance of stubble even until spring passage time) or near to the stone wall where the path divides. They sometimes even perch obligingly on the wall or the wire above it allowing clear identification without having to resort to a telescope. Again early on in the day is usually most rewarding especially for witnessing the male twite in his song flight. **Linnets** may also be present confusing the issue but providing a useful opportunity for comparison if a good view can be sustained. The most challenging situation is in late summer when mixed flocks may contain young birds of both species.

Whilst in the area at springtime the nearby patches of woodland, such as that at Barley, are worth investigating for **redstart** and **wood warbler** besides the commoner woodland species.

Index of Bird Species

All page numbers refer to the site under which the species is listed.

Useful Contacts

Lancashire Wildlife Trust
Cuerden Park Wildlife Centre
Shady Lane, Bamber Bridge
Preston PR5 6AU
Tel. 0772 324129

Royal Society for the Protection of Birds
The Lodge, Sandy
Bedfordshire, SG19 2DL
Tel. 0767 680551

The Wildfowl & Wetlands Trust
Slimbridge, Gloucester, GL2 7BT
Tel. 0453 890333

British Trust for Ornithology
The National Centre for Ornithology
The Nunnery, Thetford
Norfolk, IP24 2PU
Tel. 0842 750050

Birdline Northwest
For the latest regional bird news ring
0891 700 249.
This line is charged at a premium rate
which at the time of writing was 39p
per minute at cheap rate and 48.5p
per minute at other times (including
VAT).